The Ethics Bowl Way

The Ethics Bowl Way

Answering Questions, Questioning Answers, and Creating Ethical Communities

Edited by

Roberta Israeloff
Karen Mizell

ROWMAN & LITTLEFIELD
Lanham • Boulder • New York • London

Published by Rowman & Littlefield
An imprint of The Rowman & Littlefield Publishing Group, Inc.
4501 Forbes Boulevard, Suite 200, Lanham, Maryland 20706
www.rowman.com

86-90 Paul Street, London EC2A 4NE, United Kingdom

Copyright © 2022 by Roberta Israeloff and Karen Mizell

All rights reserved. No part of this book may be reproduced in any form or by any electronic or mechanical means, including information storage and retrieval systems, without written permission from the publisher, except by a reviewer who may quote passages in a review.

British Library Cataloguing in Publication Information Available

Library of Congress Cataloging-in-Publication Data

Names: Israeloff, Roberta, 1952– editor. | Mizell, Karen, 1952– editor.
Title: The Ethics Bowl way : answering questions, questioning answers, and creating ethical communities / edited by Roberta Israeloff, Karen Mizell.
Description: Lanham : Rowman & Littlefield, [2022] | Series: Big ideas for young thinkers | Includes bibliographical references. | Summary: "Ethics Bowl espouses a new way to engage in discussions about complex ethical issues"— Provided by publisher.
Identifiers: LCCN 2022003970 (print) | LCCN 2022003971 (ebook) | ISBN 9781475861617 (cloth) | ISBN 9781475861624 (paperback) | ISBN 9781475861631 (epub)
Subjects: LCSH: Debates and debating. | Ethics.
Classification: LCC PN4181 .E74 2022 (print) | LCC PN4181 (ebook) | DDC 808.53—dc23/eng/20220318
LC record available at https://lccn.loc.gov/2022003970
LC ebook record available at https://lccn.loc.gov/2022003971

*With gratitude to Bob Ladenson
for writing a lesson plan that turned into Ethics
Bowl and enriching the lives of so many,
we dedicate this book to the enduring legacy of Pat Croskery,
who always listened.*

"Ethics Bowl is sports for nerds, and it's glorious."—High School Ethics Bowler

"It ain't what you don't know that gets you into trouble. It's what you know for sure that just ain't so."—Mark Twain

Contents

Foreword ... xi
   Thomas E. Wartenberg, Series Editor

Preface ... xiii

Acknowledgments ... xvii

PART I: ETHICS BOWL BASICS ... 1

Chapter 1: The Ideal of an Ethical Community ... 3
   Robert F. Ladenson

Chapter 2: Debating Democracy: Building Argument Programs for Good Citizenship ... 11
   Kyle Robertson

Chapter 3: Optional but Suggested: The Role of Ethical Theory and Research in Ethics Bowl Preparation ... 19
   Richard Greene

PART II: BEST PRACTICES ... 27

Chapter 4: Values in Ethics Bowl Design ... 29
   Jeanine DeLay

Chapter 5: The Enduring Rewards of Ethics Bowl Case Writing ... 39
   Peggy Connolly

Chapter 6: Coaching: Winning Isn't Everything ... 49
   Marcia A. McKelligan

Chapter 7: Listening Well: Judging an Ethics Bowl ... 57
   Wendy C. Turgeon

Chapter 8: Beyond Argument: Learning Life Skills through Ethics Bowl   65
Andrew Cullison

Chapter 9: Room for All: Inclusivity and the High School Ethics Bowl   73
Jana Mohr Lone

PART III: EXPANDING THE REACH OF ETHICS BOWL   81

Chapter 10: The "Turn to Reason": Ethics Bowl in the Classroom   83
William M. Beals, Christina Drogalis, and Morgan E. Wallhagen

Chapter 11: Deliberating across the Lifespan   91
Michael Vazquez

Chapter 12: Ethics Bowl at San Quentin   101
Connie Krosney and Kathleen J. Richards

Chapter 13: Meeting the Challenge: The Future of Ethics Bowl   111
Alex M. Richardson

Chapter 14: From Ethics Bowler to Coach: Lifelong Learning through Ethics Bowl   119
Rachel Robison-Greene

Appendix: Sample High School Ethics Bowl Case and Study Questions   125

Notes   127

References and Resources   131

About the Editors and Contributors   137

Foreword

Thomas E. Wartenberg, Series Editor

Ethics Bowls have emerged as one of the most successful ways of introducing students to the study of ethics and, more generally, philosophy itself. Thousands of students participate in Ethics Bowls each year. By doing so, they learn a great deal about ethics, but not by studying the ideas put forward by philosophers about the nature of our values. Instead, they learn about ethics by working together with others to figure out what they think about a range of ethical case studies they are asked to consider as well as why they think what they do. This has proven to be a great way to get students to take ethics—and philosophy—seriously.

The authors of the fourteen chapters comprising *The Ethics Bowl Way* present various important features of Ethics Bowls. Although the program began as a way to introduce college students to ethical thinking, it has morphed in a number of different directions. From the contributions to this book, in addition to learning about college level Ethics Bowls, we find out that the program has been expanded into high schools and even more recently middle schools. In addition, Ethics Bowls have taken place in prisons and senior centers as the fruitfulness of this model has led to innovative uses of the basic model.

What the authors make clear is that the widely shared assumption that Ethics Bowls are a form of competitive intellectual activity is not accurate. The participants on an Ethics Bowl team are, of course, interested in winning the competitions in which they are engaged, but the primary focus of Ethics Bowls is on a cooperative learning process that is achieved through focusing on specific cases that have complex ethical aspects to them. They argue that Ethics Bowls promote many specific intellectual virtues that students often lack—and that our society is sorely in need of. Among them are empathy, thoughtfulness, and compassion.

The chapters in this book are written in a very accessible and readable style. They contain both theoretical discussions of the virtues of the Ethics Bowl model, discussions of specific ways in which Ethics Bowls have functioned, and a great deal of practical advice for anyone thinking about taking part in an Ethics Bowl as a participant, coach, or judge. I expect this book to become the "go-to" handbook for anyone interested in Ethics Bowls.

Preface

Curiosity led us both to stumble into Ethics Bowl.

For professional reasons, and several years apart, we found ourselves attending the annual conference of the Association for Practical and Professional Ethics. When Karen first attended, she had just been hired to teach philosophy at a large, open-enrollment university with a General Education Ethics course. Roberta, the director of the newly launched Squire Family Foundation that promoted philosophy education in elementary and secondary schools, found her way to the conference a few years later. Both of us were intrigued to learn that something called the Intercollegiate Ethics Bowl would be taking place as part of the program, and wandered into a match not knowing what to expect.

You may not know much about Ethics Bowl or what to expect to learn about it in this book either. Simply put, Ethics Bowl is a nuanced variation of debate. Teams are not assigned "pro" or "con" roles but rather take turns discussing their positions on timeless and timely ethical dilemmas (that they have analyzed and prepared in advance of the Bowl). Although the event is competitive, it's also collegial: the teams try to win by helping each other and by thinking more deeply, systematically, and rigorously about their arguments. Flexible rather than entrenched thinking is rewarded; depth of understanding rather than rhetorical flourishes win the day.

This brief explanation, however, doesn't begin to convey the magnetic pull Ethics Bowl exerts on just about everyone who experiences it. Its power doesn't come through even in videos—you have to witness it live, as we did. What stuck in our minds long after the event was over wasn't the precise format, the cases, the participating teams, or who won. Instead, we remember the nature and quality of the engagement that gripped all of us in the standing-room-only ballroom in which the Bowl's final match unfolded. The audience, riveted, hung on every word with laser-like focus, approving or frowning as members of the teams advanced their arguments, smiling, grimacing, and biting its nails as the judges scored the match.

When the winning team was announced, we all jumped to our feet, high fives, applause, and shouts rippling through the room. On stage, the winners received their trophy, the teams shook hands with each other, with the judges, the moderator, and their coaches. Amazingly, the room remained packed and abuzz. It was nearly 11 p.m., but the conversation didn't stop. Groups of people congregated in the aisles and near the exit, their reviews and critiques of the match spilling, finally, into the lobby and continuing in the hotel elevators. The next morning, I heard people talking about it over breakfast in the hotel restaurant. Neither Karen nor I had ever seen anything like it.

Karen recalls that this contrasted sharply with her experience teaching a mandatory ethics class, in which students were reluctant to focus on the subject, and which led her to feel as if she were Sisyphus pushing a boulder uphill. After seeing an Ethics Bowl in action, it was clear to her that she had found a powerful tool to facilitate student learning. Returning home, she recruited and coached a team that was invited to participate at the next IEB.

In time, she introduced Ethics Bowl to high schools in her area, an innovation that caught Roberta's attention. She had been looking for a way to bring philosophy into K–12 classrooms since it is not routinely taught there. Philosophy can prove an intimidating word, but most everyone has an idea of what "ethics" entails. Maybe this particular branch of philosophy would prove the portal through which many students and teachers could approach the discipline.

The idea caught on. As we write this note, the Ethics Bowl—which began as a humble classroom exercise—has traveled across the country and around the world. In 2020, APPE IEB sponsored twelve regional Ethics Bowls involving over 150 colleges and universities; over two hundred teams participated aided by over five hundred volunteer moderators, coaches, and judges. In 2021, the National High School Ethics Bowl (NHSEB), which began in 2012, hosted forty-one regionals in over thirty states involving about four thousand students. And the newest entry, the Middle School Ethics Bowl, was launched in 2018. Internationally, Bowls (including adaptations of the program) have been launched in Canada, Australia, and the UK.

Thanks to our generous contributors, you will read about all this and more in the pages that follow. You'll also see that the Ethics Bowl, and the community that sustains it, is unique. As Karen notes, in the over twenty years in which she has been involved, everyone—organizers, hosts, coaches, judges, and moderators—is deeply motivated to help students navigate the ethical complexities and ambiguities of our time and to cultivate ethical discernment. The goal is to help participants acknowledge the ethical snarls that confront us all and to engage in discourse that investigates their own and others' ethical perplexities. Through dialogue, they confront ethical entanglements, deliberate the essential rightness or goodness of their own and others' positions, and sometimes consider consequences to stakeholders.

The pedagogical component often involves explaining basic ethical theory and applied ethics to prepare for the event. From this rudimentary introduction, students ideally develop their own positions and applications. When weighing the teams' arguments, the panel of judges, composed of scholars, professionals, and community members, has the opportunity to converse about ethical insights, probe the teams' ethical judgment, and generally advance the ethical conversation.

We hope this book—more encompassing than a primer but surely not as inclusive as it could have been—will also help advance the ethical conversation. Its three parts—Ethics Bowl basics, best practices, and potential—will, we hope, introduce Ethics Bowl to readers who aren't yet aware of it; create new fans; and inspire those already in the community to experiment, innovate, and make the event ever more challenging, fair, adaptable, and diverse.

In addition to the authors who generously contributed their time and expertise to help compose this book, we reached out to the growing network of High School Ethics Bowlers, Intercollegiate Ethics Bowlers, and alumni. You will find their very eloquent reflections on Ethics Bowl sometimes within, and always at the end of, each chapter. These testimonials all speak to what we most value about Ethics Bowl—that it induces us all to critically listen; to be open to and to consider other points of view; to put ourselves in another's shoes; to speak and be heard, respectfully; to have our assertions as well as our questions, doubts, and uncertainties honored.

Acknowledgments

An edited book is a dialogue, a multiperson collaboration. Together, we thank our contributors, who carved time out of their busy schedules and multiple obligations to help produce this book. We're grateful for all the conversations we had along the way.

Roberta would like to thank the loyal, dedicated, enthusiastic, supportive Long Island High School Ethics Bowl community—students, judges, moderators, and especially our exemplary coaches who put their hearts and souls into the event: Will Bertolotti, Brad Brummeler, Lori Christensen, Andrea Darbee, Phil Edelson, Lydia Esslinger, Jim Hughes, Bryan Krahel, Joyce Mennona, Dana Mollica, Sean Riley, Deb Surian, Jennifer Theo-Kupstas, Wendy Way, Allyson Weseley, and Jeremy Zylbert. For fifteen years, you've kept our Bowl—an engine of innovation—alive and vital. Thanks as well to Kathleen Wallace, and Johanna Farrell and Denise Deputy, our partners at Hofstra University; Tom Wartenberg, Tom Koerner, Carlie Wall, and Jessica McCleary. She also thanks Gary Squire, Brian Shrag, Matt Deaton (the Johnny Appleseed of High School Ethics Bowl), Ariel Sykes, Dave Ventresca, Karen Rezach, and the original, devoted, undeterred team of NHSEB founders: Jan Boxill, Kate Fanfani, Katelin Shaw Kaiser, and Adam Schaefer.

Karen thanks Richard Greene, Bob and Joanne Ladenson, Jeffrey Nielsen, Rachel Robison-Greene, Lisa Lambert, and the many students, friends, and faculty who stepped up to judge, moderate, and attend to the many little details of the events, including serving pizza to participants. She is also truly grateful to her children, Emory, Kendall, and Collin, who patiently helped prepare, organize, and administer Ethics Bowl events every year for over a decade as they progressed from high school to college graduation.

PART I

Ethics Bowl Basics

Chapter 1

The Ideal of an Ethical Community

Robert F. Ladenson

In 1993, Dr. Robert Ladenson created the Ethics Bowl as a classroom activity when he was a professor of philosophy at Illinois Institute of Technology. That it outgrew the confines of the classroom so quickly, expanding into an intramural, statewide, regional, and ultimately national and even international event, speaks not only to its popularity among students and faculty but also its enduring value as a way to encourage people to talk about controversial issues within trusting, respectful communities. In this chapter, Dr. Ladenson discusses why he was motivated to create Ethics Bowl, its goals, and guiding principles. As many of its participants agree, Ethics Bowl couldn't be more timely.

* * *

Ethics Bowl is a competitive yet collaborative event in which teams of students discuss real-life ethical issues. In each round of the event, teams take turns analyzing cases about complex ethical dilemmas and responding to questions and comments from the other team and from a panel of judges. Ethics Bowl differs from a debate in that students are not assigned opposing views; rather, they defend whichever position they think is correct, provide each other with constructive criticism, and win by demonstrating that they have thought rigorously and systematically about the cases and engaged respectfully and supportively with all participants.

The goal of Ethics Bowl is to do more than teach students how to think through ethical issues: it is to teach students how to think through ethical issues *together*, as fellow citizens in a complex ethical and political community.

FORMAT, PROCEDURES, AND RULES

Over the years since its inception, the Ethics Bowl has been adapted in various ways (Ethics Bowl innovations will be discussed in part III). Most of the changes involve varying the length of time teams have to confer and speak, point designation, number of rounds, and number of cases discussed. However, the basic format, as outlined below, remains the same.

In an Ethics Bowl match a moderator asks two teams of three to five students questions that pose ethical problems over areas such as social/political topics (war and peace, freedom of expression, economic justice, health care); the classroom (plagiarism or other kinds of cheating in an academic context); personal relationships (dating, friendship); and professional ethics (engineering, business, medicine, law). [Editors' note: See the appendix for a sample Ethics Bowl case and study questions.]

Each of the two teams in an ethics bowl match is asked a different question, which each team answers according to the following format: the moderator poses a question to Team A, which then has two minutes to confer, after which it must state its answer (in no more than ten minutes). Team A does not respond cold, however. Six weeks prior to the competition, all of the competing teams receive a set of cases that presents ethical issues upon which the questions a team may be called upon to answer at the Ethics Bowl are based.

When Team A has completed the presentation of its answer, Team B has one minute to confer, after which it comments (for no more than five minutes) upon Team A's answer to the moderator's question. Team A then receives one minute to confer, after which it responds (for no more than five minutes) to Team B's commentary.

A panel of three judges then poses questions to Team A to elicit the team's viewpoint on important aspects of the question or to seek clarification in regard to the team's responses to points made by the commenting team. The judges, who are highly qualified persons in diverse fields, receive advance copies of the cases upon which questions are based at the same time as the student participants, about six weeks before the Ethics Bowl competition.

The same format is then repeated with the two teams exchanging roles. That is to say, Team B becomes the presenting team, and Team A becomes the commenting team. Team B's question is based upon a different case than the one upon which Team A's question was based. After the judges have concluded their questions to Team B, the moderator asks the three judges to indicate their respective evaluations of each team's presentation and commentary. Prior to the competition, the judges have been instructed as to the criteria they are to apply in their evaluations.

BASIC EDUCATIONAL OBJECTIVES OF THE ETHICS BOWL

Many issues students face during both their high school and their undergraduate college experience, as well as many they will confront in their future life experiences, have the following characteristics: they not only are complex and controversial but also difficult to resolve in virtue of implicating basic questions that cannot be resolved conclusively about human nature, the nature of society, and/or comparative evaluation of benefits and harms.

Such applies in the case of topics such as cheating, plagiarism, personal relationships, gender equality, and campus social or political controversies, as well as issues of professional ethics, which may come into play in their future careers. The same point applies in regard to issues upon which they surely will need to deliberate for exercising their rights, meeting their responsibilities, and furthering the ideals of membership in the American democratic body politics.

Education on both the levels of high school and college can make the following three valuable and distinctive contributions to the development of a student's capabilities relative to ethical reasoning and judgment, especially in connection with complex, controversial, highly viewpoint-dependent and difficult-to-resolve issues.

1. It can help students develop a framework of analysis for addressing ethical issues in an intellectually well-organized manner.
2. It can provide an opportunity for students to acquire valuable information relative to arriving at judgments about ethical issues of special importance to them in light of their respective interests, concerns, and career aspirations.
3. It can foster the capacity for ethical understanding.

The last of the above items—the capacity for ethical understanding—needs further words of elucidation. The positions people take on important, but complex, controversial, highly viewpoint-dependent, and difficult-to-resolve ethical issues tend to depend strongly upon factors such as an individual's politics, personal values, gender, or religion. Even from the standpoint of moral philosophies that posit objective standards of ethical reasoning, no one reasonably may assume that his or her judgments about such issues proceed from a neutral standpoint uninfluenced by the above kinds of factors.

A question thus arises of what ethical understanding means relative to complex, controversial, highly viewpoint-dependent, and difficult-to-resolve issues. I believe that it consists largely of viewing from inside other ethical positions besides those with which a person agrees. It involves not only awareness of the arguments advanced on behalf of those positions but also understanding of the concerns that motivate the arguments, and even to some extent, an appreciation of their force.

Development of the capacity for ethical understanding relative to complex, controversial, highly viewpoint-dependent, and difficult-to-resolve issues thus only can take place on a large scale in societies where a strong and effective right of free speech exists. The existence of a strong and effective right of free speech in society, however, although necessary in this regard, is far from sufficient. In the case of the above-mentioned kinds of issues, a person's capacity of ethical understanding tends to develop most readily in an environment with three special characteristics:

1. A person feels strongly motivated to state her views on the issues.
2. They feel strongly motivated also to listen carefully to what others have to say about their views on the issues.
3. Everyone involved in discussing the issues is motivated strongly to do so in a way that brings out clearly the similarities and differences in outlook among the discussant's views.

The Ethics Bowl, I believe, is a form of experiential education that seeks to create a learning environment in which students can develop crucial capabilities for the attainment of ethical understanding in regard to complex, controversial, highly viewpoint-dependent, and difficult-to-resolve ethical issues. These crucial capacities are open-mindedness; willingness and readiness to engage in meaningful conversation; and deliberative thoughtfulness and open-mindedness.

As noted earlier, six weeks before an Ethics Bowl competition takes place, the participating teams receive a set of ethics cases. Each case is about one single-spaced typed page. The teams are not given questions about the cases. Instead they have to identify key ethical issues themselves and develop a team position for each case, which they then must be able to state clearly and to justify. All the cases pose complex, controversial, highly viewpoint-dependent, and difficult-to-resolve issues. Teams cannot quickly reach full agreement among team members on most, let alone all, of the cases.

A team's challenge thus is to identify key ethical issues raised by the cases and then to work out positions on them that every team member agrees are reasonable in the sense that an ethically conscientious person could accept them after careful consideration. To do so, each team member must be able to listen to the others with an open mind, to consider seriously views that may differ from their own, and to appreciate the force of such different views in the sense of acknowledging that an ethically responsible person could accept them.

WILLINGNESS AND READINESS TO ENGAGE IN MEANINGFUL COMMUNICATION

The procedural format of an Ethics Bowl match described above raises an apparent question. What happens if the commenting team agrees with the presenting team's answer to the moderator's question? Here is the answer. Ethics Bowl cases, without fail, are conceptually deep and factually complex. The likelihood is vanishingly small that a team's answer to a moderator's question will leave the opposing team absolutely speechless so that the presenting team need not say anything in response.

To the contrary, a commenting team may indicate that it agrees with the presenting team's answer and then discuss aspects of the justifying argument presented that it finds problematic. Furthermore, even if the commenting team considers the presenting team's argument persuasive, it may wish to develop another justifying argument that highlights other ethically significant considerations in the case, because no ethical issue in an Ethics Bowl case can be closed completely, as contrasted with being settled for immediate practical purposes. The mark of an excellent commentary is the contribution it makes to continuing a mutually beneficial discussion.

DELIBERATIVE THOUGHTFULNESS

Ethics Bowl judges are required to apply three criteria. The first is clarity, and the second is thoroughness. The third concerns deliberative thoughtfulness in a sense essential to ethical understanding in connection with the kinds of issues posed in Ethics Bowl cases. In this context, ethical understanding thus consists largely of understanding the views of people with whom one disagrees. It means not simply awareness of what they've said or written but calls also for serious effort to understand their views from the inside—to comprehend the key concerns motivating them and, at least to some extent, appreciate their force.

Prepping and training efforts for judges thus emphasize the critical importance of posing questions to teams in a match that probes the team members' depth of ethical understanding in regard to views different from the ones they've presented in discussing the cases they consider. Correspondingly, a key part of an Ethics Bowl team's preparation and coaching involves trying to anticipate questions.

With respect to judges' questions, it becomes apparent when observing Ethics Bowl matches that most of the time the concerns underlying these questions were identified and discussed carefully by the teams in their preparations for the competition. Students attest, however, that frequently they have been challenged, with great educational benefit, by judges' questions, which approached cases from different directions than those they considered, or that pursued the students' lines of reasoning to deeper levels than they reached in their discussions prior to the competition.

ETHICS BOWL AND THE IDEAL OF ETHICAL COMMUNITY

What accounts for the Ethics Bowl's long-standing popularity? Here is a hypothesis that increasingly has seemed plausible to me over the more than a quarter century since my colleagues in the Center for the Study of Ethics in the Professions at the Illinois Institute of Technology and I organized the first Ethics Bowl competition. In any event, the hypothesis, I believe, is crucial in my own case—that is, for understanding what motivated me to devote as much time and effort as I did over so many years to organizing and developing the Ethics Bowl.

The Ethics Bowl meets a vital yet chronically underaddressed need. It develops capabilities and dispositions that must be widespread for American democracy to flourish. Even more broadly, such development is indispensable for the United States, and indeed the entire world, to approach the ideal of ethical community, understood in a way most relevant to the lives of human beings as lived in any social environment.

Ethics Bowl models an ideal of ethical community under which the following virtues of discourse concerning contentious ethical issues are shared widely:

1. Willingness to listen to expressions of viewpoints different from one's own on complex, controversial, highly viewpoint-dependent, and difficult-to-resolve ethical issues
2. To give such viewpoints careful consideration
3. To discuss the viewpoints in ways that combine candor with restraint and mutual respect

Such an ideal of ethical community—focusing upon virtues of discourse on ethical issues likely to generate strong feelings liable to result in bitter conflict—although difficult to realize, does not lie beyond the reach of human capability and is neither elitist nor culture bound. To the contrary, open-mindedness, willingness to listen, and mutual respect are intrinsic to sound reasoning about ethical issues for anyone who possesses the cognitive and volitional abilities necessary to make an ethical judgment.

Here is one among many salient examples of the preceding points. Several years ago, a colleague from the Illinois Tech Center for the Study of Ethics in the Professions and I conducted an hour-and-a-half Ethics Bowl workshop for a group of high school students. The workshop took place at the Illinois Tech campus on a Saturday morning. The students, all African American, were from a public high school located in the Pullman area on the southeast side of Chicago, a low-income and, in other ways, struggling community.

When the workshop session, which had gone very well, ended, one of the teachers who had accompanied the students to the Illinois Tech campus that morning posed two questions to them. First, did the students think they had learned anything of value about how best to discuss with others complex and contentious ethical issues? They all agreed that they had. Second, the teacher asked how they thought they would have discussed the Ethics Bowl cases we had given them to consider if my colleague and I hadn't prepped and coached them on the Ethics Bowl format. One student responded, with the others nodding in agreement emphatically, that "Probably we would have wound up just shouting at each other."

Since creating the Ethics Bowl in 1993, I have received many (probably several hundred) communications that are overwhelmingly positive from students, educators, and other persons who have either taken part in or observed an Ethics Bowl match. The range of the different personal backgrounds and institutional affiliations among such persons has been immense. (It includes, for example, faculty members at prestigious American colleges and inmates at San Quentin prison, where I had the powerful experience of being one of the judges in an Ethics Bowl match between a team of San Quentin inmates and the University of California, Santa Cruz, Ethics Bowl team.)

The most reinforcing aspect of these communications, by far, has been the extent to which, like the response of the student from the Pullman neighborhood, the thoughts expressed in the communications track closely the conception of the Ethics Bowl's basic educational objective set forth in this chapter.

The ideal of ethical community the Ethics Bowl models has resonated powerfully with students and educators now for over a quarter century. One could not reasonably ask for stronger encouragement to continue efforts on both the undergraduate college and precollegiate levels to further the growth and flourishing of the Ethics Bowl.

* * *

Without a doubt, participating in the Ethics Bowl has been the most influential component of my formative years. The hours spent seated (and occasionally pacing) in a high school classroom, engaged in thoughtful dialogue with my peers, made me who I am today. Even though only a dozen students participated in the ethics program at my high school, the Bowl had a ripple effect throughout the building: the conversations flowed outside of the classroom's confines, spreading around the school. I didn't even have my driver's license yet, and there I was, applying Aristotelian theories and Kantian principles to modern society's biggest issues. What I appreciated the most was that our coach and the Ethics Bowl's judges never discounted me or my reasoning because of my age. I am grateful to have had such an experience where I was seen and heard by adults and treated as one. It's why I participate as a moderator and judge now. All young people should have access to this type of philosophical education.

—Jillian Leavey, High School Ethics Bowl alumnus

Chapter 2

Debating Democracy

Building Argument Programs for Good Citizenship

Kyle Robertson

Ethics Bowl resembles debate in several ways: two teams face each other in front of a panel of judges, take turns speaking about controversial issues, and receive scores for their performances. In fact, one may wonder why there was a need for another such format. But listen closely, and key differences emerge. Ethics Bowlers do not value winning at any price; instead, they know that they need to display intellectual rigor, curiosity, and open-mindedness. In short, they value collaborating and challenging each other to reach a deeper truth, a building block of deliberative democracy. In this chapter, philosopher Dr. Kyle Robertson, veteran Ethics Bowl coach and judge, discusses the essential differences between Ethics Bowl and debate with an eye toward developing habits of responsible citizenship.

* * *

Debating teams are promoted in schools as a spur to effective language and incisive thought. They serve that purpose, but only by setting the goal of persuasion above the goal of truth. The debater's strength lies not in intellectual curiosity nor in amenability to rational persuasion by others, but in his skill in defending a preconception come what may.—Quine, W.V.O., *Quiddities: an Intermittently Philosophical Dictionary*. Harvard University Press, 1987, p. 183.

If you're concerned about the effect Quine is talking about (and you should be), then Ethics Bowl may appeal to you as an alternative format that offers many of the benefits of forensic debate without some of these problems. (I am using forensic debate to refer to Lincoln-Douglas, parliamentary, and policy debate formats but the qualities of debate discussed below pertain to other forms of debate as well.) I aim to convince you that the Ethics Bowl provides such an alternative, and to provide you with arguments you can use, supporting the switch to your own students, community members, and administrators.

Put simply, Ethics Bowl is a formal argument format that refuses to put the goal of persuasion above the goal of truth, or at least the honest pursuit of a better answer. Ethics Bowl does not reward teams for persuading the judging panel to agree with their answer; they are rewarded for persuading the judges that they are thoughtfully pursuing an answer to the difficult applied ethical issues in front of them. This relatively modest shift in focus profoundly affects the experience of students participating in an Ethics Bowl.

The differences between Ethics Bowl and forensic debate styles are linked to the values a program teaching formal, oral argumentation serves in society. Argument plays a foundational role in deliberative democracies, such as our own, so the beliefs we share about what makes a good argument are constitutive of how our democracy functions. How we choose to teach in our schools about this topic—that is, how we choose to construct an educational argumentation program—is therefore also a choice about what sort of a democracy we want to live in. If you are concerned, as I am, about what passes for a good argument in our culture, you should worry about how we teach our students to argue.

ADVERSARIAL V. DIALOGIC ARGUMENTS

The distinction between a forensic debate and an Ethics Bowl roughly parallels the distinction between arguing to beat an adversary and arguing to get better answers. I am going to call these two types of argument adversarial and dialogic, respectively, and show that the different goals of each give rise to dramatically different debate programs.

I want to note, however, that although there is disagreement in the Ethics Bowl community about whether or not Ethics Bowl is a "debate" format, I think it is best understood as a form of debate if we focus on the ways in which all debate programs inculcate norms of argumentation that influence our everyday notions of what good democratic deliberation looks like.

We model adversarial debate programs on the activity of lawyers in a courtroom where the adversarial model reigns supreme. Many terms used in the forensic debate world are directly linked to legal contexts. "Forensic" generally refers to the type of examination that happens in a courtroom, and forensic debate uses notions of affirmative and negative arguments and cross-examination, for example. But the influence goes deeper than language. In American courts, two adversarial parties fight over not just questions of ultimate guilt and responsibility but also over basic factual questions (in discovery) and interpretive legal questions (at all stages of litigation).

These fights are transparently partisan; it's not uncommon for one lawyer to argue diametrically opposed factual or legal claims at different points in the case, depending on which interpretation benefits their client at a given stage. This is indicative of adversarial formats: you are trying to conquer the other person in order to win. Achieving truth or even constructing a good argument is only a means to that end. You can win an adversarial argument by showing the other person made a mistake or failed to carry their burden of proof; or by making a point that could be false but was left unrefuted. Adversarial arguments are zero-sum, in that any good points made by one side count against the other side. Because there is no way to build a constructive position together, each party constantly tries to undermine its opponent.

This adversarial model is familiar to anyone who watches TV or reads the newspaper; it is used by pundits and politicians, in political arguments on internet comment threads, and on social media. This style of argument is so ubiquitous that, for many, it defines the term *argument*. But there are alternatives.

In contrast, dialogic argument functions as an important part of a healthy, deliberative democracy. Its norms are grounded in communication, respect, and mutual understanding and progress rather than domination. Dialogic arguments are common in excellent academic contexts, and in good philosophy discussions in particular. It is a form of collective decision-making through conversation, and a healthy way of managing one's own beliefs.[1]

To further contrast these two argument models, think about the different roles of lawyer and juror, and the qualities each needs to do a good job. Good lawyers argue adversarially, and they are important but only in certain contexts. When the force of the state is against you in criminal court, you want a specialized adversarial advocate to stand up for you. But as a good juror, you need to collaborate, reserving judgment through the process of an open-minded, unbiased examination of evidence. These features are inconsistent with the adversarial style of argument. It seems to me that we have all fashioned ourselves as lawyers for our own political teams, and everyday political discussion has widely devolved into adversarial combat.

So what does a dialogic argument look like? First, it is collaborative. The parties work together to create their arguments and genuinely care about the perspectives and insights of others. Healthy democracies must be able to grapple with the pluralism of moral views in their population, and so argument as a practice of collective decision-making must respect alternative viewpoints and competing notions of the good life.

Second, dialogic argument is truth-seeking and encourages honesty. Participants are incentivized to show good thinking and insight, and rewarded for making each other's answers better. For argument to function as a means of decision-making, it must aim at an external end beyond simply beating opponents. That end, in a healthy democracy, is good policy decision-making. Dialogic argument values good answers more than appearances of cleverness or moral righteousness and eschews, or at least de-emphasizes, gamesmanship.

Third, dialogic argument encourages open-mindedness. Participants must wrestle with the possibility that they may be wrong and fully understand the reasons why. They need to engage with alternative points of view as real possibilities. Participants should see their opponents as epistemic and moral peers—that is, as people with a similar capacity to reason well about what is true and what is moral—and interpret opposing points of view charitably. Dialogic argument asks us to embrace humility, understanding that everyone's viewpoint and knowledge base is always limited, partial, and potentially biased.

In short, dialogic debate is collaborative, truth-seeking, honest, and open-minded. The Ethics Bowl seeks to embody dialogic argument, and I think that these features capture most of what is good about Ethics Bowl and most of what makes it worth trying. (Actual Ethics Bowl competitions, norms, and rules may skew from this notion of dialogic argument, but there is room within the format to improve and reform the event to make it better. My notion of dialogic argument here is more of a regulative ideal for Ethics Bowl than a strict description of the event.)

In Ethics Bowl, you win a round by showing the judges that you've thought more deeply and broadly about the ethical issues at stake. You do that by engaging in a constructive dialogue with the opposing team and the judges about the case. Although it can be important to point out errors of reasoning in order to deliberate well, focusing on the mistakes of others does not earn teams many points. Instead, in a well-judged Ethics Bowl, teams naturally begin to embrace the norms of dialogic argument.

SEEKING TRUTH TOGETHER

I would now like to offer two more concrete arguments for the benefits of a dialogic style of argument over the forensic model. First, I'll expand upon the notion that because the Ethics Bowl enhances the intellectual skills we should want to inculcate in our citizens, it is a good model to be adopted by schools. Next, I'll argue that dialogic argument better addresses some of the psychological challenges we face when we want to reason well. Adversarial argument, unfortunately, often exacerbates our tendency to reason poorly, and therefore is more potentially harmful to our democratic deliberation than it might at first appear.

Learning to argue well could be good for us in two ways: intrinsically, because it's a valuable skill *in and of itself*, or extrinsically (instrumentally), because it enables us to achieve external goals that are good in themselves. This subtle distinction may seem trivial, but it matters deeply because of two related truths. First, the ability to argue well is intrinsically important to the health of our deliberative democracy. Argument is the means by which we engage in pluralistic decision-making, and democratic decision-making flounders when we are unable to engage with each other across our disagreements and make important choices. Healthy argumentative habits may even be important to our own epistemic and cognitive health.[2]

The second truth is that forensic debate programs only make sense if we value argument instrumentally, not intrinsically. That is, the argumentative skills we learn in forensic debate are not the ones on which a healthy democracy depends.

To think about whether argument is intrinsically or instrumentally valuable, consider this question: Is argument more like learning to read and write or learning to play basketball? Both activities are valuable. We need to teach reading and writing in school because human flourishing, particularly in our complex society, inherently involves communicating ideas with each other in written form and understanding and navigating the complexity of texts and other written media around us.

On the other hand, basketball is also a valuable activity but not in the same way. We don't need to be able to throw a ball through a hoop to succeed as a human. Learning to play is valuable because it can teach us other skills and habits that are generally useful for our flourishing, such as appreciating the values of discipline, effort, and teamwork. And it is fun! But basketball and other organized sports are important educationally because of their extrinsic rather than intrinsic value.

Forensic speech and debate programs treat argument more like basketball and not enough like reading and writing. By this I mean that learning adversarial argument is not necessary for human flourishing. Acquiring the skill may help certain adults find good employment; excellent forensic debaters, for example, may become excellent attorneys. But most adults in our society wouldn't appreciate arguing with each other as if they were opponents in a debate. Think of it this way: it would be absurd to justify stealing a basketball out of the hands of a stranger you passed on the street by claiming that it's a good move on the basketball court. It's just as absurd to treat a casual assertion in friendly conversation as an opportunity to conduct an adversarial argument.

Like basketball and other sports, learning forensic debate skills has extrinsic value: they teach students the value of teamwork, sportsmanship, and emotional regulation. Students also can learn to master rhetorical and research skills that can help them become better public speakers. But forensic debate skills are no more essential to leading a well-lived life than learning to shoot baskets.

But forensic debate skills are not just inessential; they can also be seen as counterproductive. By this I mean that when we adopt the adversarial rather than deliberative debate, we may be systematically chipping away at the very idea of productive civic engagement, and encouraging bad citizenship skills along the way, as you'll see below. In fact, I could diagnose our current political moment in this light. Turn on the television or go online: you'll see legislators, political pundits, and presidential candidates treating argument as sport rather than as essential to good governing.

SEEKING TRUTH FOR OURSELVES

Adversarial debate programs also run the risk of exacerbating some of our worst tendencies toward self-justification. Often, when we reason poorly, we do so to justify ourselves. This is known as "motivated reasoning," and it occurs when we reason not to seek accuracy or truth but instead to reach a desired conclusion.[3] The cognitive habits that cause us to engage in motivated reasoning may be rooted in our evolutionary history, but they poison a well-functioning democracy whose citizens should strive to use reason to determine sound policy.

It follows, then, that we should inculcate habits of mind that move us away from motivated reasoning, which is a goal of Ethics Bowl. Forensic debate, in contrast, encourages motivated reasoning because of the power of two widely known psychological phenomena: confirmation bias and cognitive dissonance.

Confirmation bias refers to the way we view new evidence. Research shows that, generally speaking, we aggressively doubt evidence that undermines our beliefs and quickly accept evidence that supports them. Thus, the better we are at arguing that new evidence isn't relevant, the stronger our confirmation bias becomes because we get better at finding reasons to doubt contrary evidence. Although not widely studied, preliminary evidence seems to indicate that training in forensic debate exacerbates our tendency to be biased toward our own prior beliefs, regardless of evidence.[4]

Cognitive dissonance refers to the lengths we will go to in order to avoid the discomfort of holding contradictory beliefs. In particular, the experience of dissonance is so unpleasant that we often drop one of the dissonant beliefs without good reason. Think of prosecutors who continue to believe that a wrongly convicted person is innocent even when confronted with overwhelming evidence to the contrary. This is cognitive dissonance at work.

Prosecutors who believe they are good at their jobs don't want to think that they could have caused an innocent person to be imprisoned. The dissonance that arises when two irreconcilable beliefs rub against each other often causes us to jettison one of these beliefs without good reason—and because we are loath to give up on the belief in our own competency, we tend to jettison the possibility that we may have made a mistake, no matter how overwhelming the exculpatory evidence.[5] Yet the ability to argue and defend any position, despite countervailing evidence, is fostered by engaging in forensic debate.

At this point, fans of forensic debating may point out that it forces you to prepare both sides of an issue. This is certainly true. Forensic debaters do need to understand different angles of argument on a case to prepare to argue either side, but they understand the different arguments as tools to use to win the debate, not pieces to craft together into a comprehensive, nuanced position. That is, the actual activity of arguing in forensic debate is not motivated by accuracy but rather by winning. In this way, forensic debate teaches that rhetorical tools, research tricks, and pieces of evidence are useful as a means to win, not a means to seeking the truth.

In fact, forensic debate often seems nihilistic, or at least agnostic, about the possibility of reaching a true or better answer to the debate question. There is even some evidence that clever people who excel at arguing are more prone to motivated reasoning. Instead of encouraging this type of faulty reasoning, we should want debate programs to inculcate in students the norms and habits of constructive dialogic argument. The norms of public reasoning in our democracy depend on the idea that debate is a means to coming to better answers to the difficult questions we face, and forensic debate undermines the good-faith attitudes we need to take to make this deliberation work.

DEMOCRATIC VIRTUE AND DELIBERATION

For all these reasons, I am an advocate for dialogic argument models and practices. However, I believe that adversarial debate has its place, specifically in contexts that we characterize as zero-sum. In criminal courts, for example, criminal defendants justifiably want and deserve attorneys who take adversarial approaches to defending their clients' freedoms. Prosecutors are not so easily justified in adversariality—they are charged with pursuing justice and truth on behalf of the state and have a moral obligation to only pursue charges they believe are warranted by the evidence (and indeed, courts recognize this to some degree by placing the *prima facie* burden of proof on the state—prosecutors don't win by simply refuting the defendant's arguments; they must bring forth affirmative proof of a crime).

But in the past fifty years, legal scholars have been asking an interesting question: Can one be a good lawyer and a good person?[6] The consensus seems to be that the answer is yes, but I mention this to note that *it was a serious debate*. That is, it is not obvious that the sorts of advocacy lawyers must regularly engage in is consistent with good moral character and good citizenship. Lawyer jokes are popular for a reason. Why, then, would we model a school extracurricular activity on an adversarial courtroom style? The answer to this question, I believe, is that we are familiar with only one style of argument. But in fact there is another model: Ethics Bowl.

No single set of techniques or debate rules will improve the health of our deliberative democracy. For that, we need to collectively buy in to a set of argumentative norms and values about what democratic deliberation can do. These values are not obvious, nor are they shared widely enough to buttress our democracy against trolls. But Ethics Bowl is an attempt to adopt and gamify those norms into a format that is based on dialogic argumentative decision-making and that embraces the values we say we most value: collaborative, truth-seeking, honest, open-minded argument.

* * *

Because the questions we face in Ethics Bowl have no easy resolution, more emphasis is placed on the thinking behind our arguments and the subsequent conversation than the results. Ethics Bowl creates a culture of open-mindedness and forces us to think for ourselves. Teams enter rounds with flexible opinions that can be reconsidered and even altered. One time, discussing the ethics of restorative discipline and its advantages and disadvantages over punitive discipline, my teammate's question prompted the opposing team to reassess its initial stance and ultimately change it. This willingness to listen and truly consider views with which you disagree strikes me as special, particularly when I see how ugly our national politics are and how many people refuse to hear opinions that contradict their own. I can also be guilty of barricading myself behind my views, and one major reason I value the Ethics Bowl is that it helps me open myself to new ideas, think critically about those ideas, and not be afraid to change my mind.

—Owen Thomas, High School Ethics Bowler

Chapter 3

Optional but Suggested

The Role of Ethical Theory and Research in Ethics Bowl Preparation

Richard Greene

We can agree that the quality of thinking Ethics Bowl promotes is central to creating an ethical community and to maintaining our democracy—but how much ethical theory do we need to know to participate in a Bowl? Do team members need to take courses in ethics? Spend hours researching the issues? The answers aren't clear cut, but in this chapter, Dr. Richard Greene offers many useful guidelines for team members, coaches, and judges.

* * *

In my twenty-plus years of involvement with the Ethics Bowl, I've worn a number of hats. I began as a coach of an intercollegiate Ethics Bowl team, but eventually began to take on more administrative roles. With Dr. Karen Mizell, I cofounded the Wasatch Regional Ethics Bowl, have served as an organizer of many competitions including regional intercollegiate competitions, high school Ethics Bowls, an intercollegiate Ethics Bowl in Kuwait, a Bioethics Bowl competition, and prison Ethics Bowls. In my capacity as director of the Intercollegiate Ethics Bowl (a position I held from 2013 to 2019), I organized the annual Intercollegiate Ethics Bowl National Competition.

One thing common to each of these experiences is that they required a training session for judges. In each of the judge training sessions, we spent much time discussing the role of outside research and the role of ethical theory in Ethics Bowl cases. Here I would like to share some of the insights I've picked up over the years. My position is that both research and ethical theory are essential to what makes Ethics Bowl among the very finest educational activities, but that each comes with its challenges and pitfalls. They are not as straightforward as one might expect at first glance.

THE ROLE OF RESEARCH

As teams begin their preparations to compete in an Ethics Bowl, they are given the fifteen or so cases that will be used in the competition. A typical Ethics Bowl case will tell a story that reveals a somewhat-balanced ethical situation, meaning that there are compelling reasons for holding a number of competing viewpoints. (It's a real virtue of the Ethics Bowl that it is not merely a hunt for the "correct" answer!) In addition to the story, a typical Ethics Bowl case will include a set of facts, which can be seen as constituting arguments for the various sides of the issues. These facts might take the form of data points, or quotations from various stakeholders, or the citing of laws, rules, or procedures, and so forth.

While these facts are useful, they do not tell the whole story. After an initial read-through of a particular case, it becomes apparent what other things a team will need to know in order to develop a solid position (i.e., a position that clearly addresses the central question raised in the case, includes all the ethically relevant information, and shows sufficient sensitivity to the fact that the case is balanced, such that it reflects a nontrivial understanding of competing viewpoints). These other things fall under the general category of outside research.

This is the type of research we're concerned with here, as opposed to other types of research an Ethics Bowler might also engage in. For example, the comments in this section do not pertain to learning about ethical theories and principles (which will come up later in the chapter), the basics of argument construction and evaluation, how to be a good public speaker, and so forth. Our concern here is the research required for specific Ethics Bowl cases.

On the one hand, outside research is never required. It is optional. On the other hand, there is an important sense in which it is frequently not truly optional. As was stated, there are times in which sorting out the ethical issues in a case just requires more than can be found in the case, and judges might come to expect a team to put in the work. This is especially true in cases that contain a lot of scientific information, or in cases that involve legal considerations, or in cases that derive from advancements in technology.

Moreover, a case may provide a team all that it needs to argue for its position, but be such that the presenting team that has not engaged in outside research may not be in a good position to address concerns raised by the opposing team during their response to the presenting team's commentary.

In short, there may be times in which a well-developed position may not be sufficient for a team to perform its very best.

STRATEGIES FOR USING RESEARCH

This, of course, bears on research strategy. It is not possible to learn everything there is to know about a set of Ethics Bowl cases in a short period of time (typical lag time between cases being released and competitions being held is around eight to ten weeks). Teams will want to make sure that their research covers the most salient facts about a case in general, as well as those facts that are salient to things they are arguing for, while balancing research against the research required for other cases and competitors' other study obligations.

In light of this, a team will want to put some thought into division of labor. On one model, which some successful teams have employed, the competitor most responsible for presenting the team's main position is the person who does the outside research for a particular case. As long as no single competitor is handling a majority of the cases, this will ensure a fair and productive division of labor. Another equally effective model has each team member doing the outside research that bears on their part of the presentation.

More recently, some teams have added a designated researcher to their team. This is a person who takes notes during practice sessions on what needs to be researched and then reports back to the team. The designated researcher does not typically compete during matches. This role is ideal for those who want to participate in the Ethics Bowl but do not want to speak publicly. Coaches often encounter situations in which they have more students who want to participate than are allowed to sit at the table during the match. Designating research roles to students can be a way of getting more students involved. This strategy can also accommodate a wider range of personalities—some students enjoy doing the preparatory work but do not enjoy public speaking. Research roles suit these students well.

In the intercollegiate Ethics Bowl there is a significant difference between regional competition cases and national competition cases. The regional case-writing committee provides a series of footnotes along with each case, but the national case-writing committee does not. This has the benefit of making preparations for the national competition a little more difficult, which seems appropriate given that only the "best of the best" make it to nationals.

Since the regional cases come with some outside research already completed, good teams will want to familiarize themselves with everything in the footnotes, if only because their competition and the judges will have done so. This may constitute the lion's share of the research to be done in preparing a case, although a team should not assume that familiarity with the footnotes in a case is sufficient.

BEST PRACTICES

Let's turn our attention to some of the dos and don'ts of outside research. First and foremost, teams should not use outside research to fundamentally change the case. This can happen in a number of ways. Sometimes teams will use outside research to dispute the facts as presented in the case. This can be appropriate, provided that doing so doesn't make the competition merely a matter of disagreements over facts. This is the Ethics Bowl, and ethical considerations need to always be at the center of the discussion. On many occasions, a team's outside research results in their arguing that the ethical issue as presented in the case does not actually exist. While this may be true, it does not release the teams from their obligations to address the central ethical question raised in the case.

Here is a useful way to think about it (and a way of thinking about it that frequently has been conveyed to judges during training sessions). Many of the Ethics Bowl cases are fictional and are designed to raise a tough ethical concern. In those cases what is expected of the participating teams is that they have a thoughtful discussion about the ethical considerations raised. Similarly, if in a nonfictional case, the actual facts (discovered via research, as opposed to those "facts" built into the case) don't generate the same ethical issues, then it's appropriate for teams to treat the case as fictional and still address the ethical issues raised.

Things can get tricky here, as sometimes the actual facts alter the ethical aspect of an issue without eliminating it. Under such circumstances teams should tread lightly and incorporate the ethical differences into their presentations in way that makes the differences explicit to the judges. So changing the ethical issue may be acceptable to some degree, but eliminating it never is.

There are also instances in which the ethical issue gets resolved between the time the set of Ethics Bowl cases is released and the competitions are held. Here it is important to not just consider what actually happened as settling the matter of what should have happened. Even though the issue has been resolved, it may not have been resolved in an optimal ethical fashion. As with the previous example, treating such cases as fictional or hypothetical seems like a good way to go; there is still an ethical issue to be addressed.

When presenting outside research, it is important to cite one's sources. In a competition the standards for citing a source are not the exacting standards one might find in an academic journal or a college term paper, but a team should be able to make it clear where their information came from (e.g.,

"In a recent article in the *New York Times*, it was reported . . . "). Moreover, teams should make it clear why the outside information is relevant to their argument. Teams should never rely on judges to figure out how their research bears on the case.

Finally, it is imperative that teams avoid using outside research to commit appeals to authority and hasty generalizations. On occasion, a team will attempt to impress the judges by citing a bunch of sources in hopes of appearing very knowledgeable or credible on a particular topic (this almost never works). If this occurs in absence of the aforementioned account of why the research is relevant to the team's argument, a lower score from the judges is the more likely result. Similarly, attempts to draw generalizations that just aren't warranted will likely result in judges looking with disfavor at a team's outside research efforts. A good rule to keep in mind: don't try to game the judges or attempt to intimidate the other team; outside research provides an opportunity to augment a case, but it should not be used to patch up or conceal a weak case.

THE ROLE OF ETHICAL THEORY

Whenever Ethics Bowl judges are trained, it is inevitable that questions pertaining to teams' use of ethical theory will arise. In fact, whether teams should be using ethical theory is one of the most divisive and controversial issues among Ethics Bowl judges. Almost every judge, once they have judged a time or two, will come to hold an opinion on the matter.

As was the case with bringing in outside research, use of ethical theory in arguing for a position is not obligatory. Nothing in the rules or the scoring rubric provided to judges requires it. When my predecessor, Dr. Patrick Croskery, was the director of the Intercollegiate Ethics Bowl, he always told judges in training, "This is the Ethics Bowl, not the ethical theory bowl." Although use of ethical theory is not obligatory, it might become obligatory given the particulars of certain Ethics Bowl cases. For example, occasionally a case will actually reference an ethical theory, or a case will just be written in such a way that judges will rightly expect that discussing a particular theory will be forthcoming.

Acceptable alternatives to using ethical theories in presenting a position might include appeal to ethical principles, such as autonomy or fairness. Under some circumstances it might make sense to support one's position by appealing to professional codes of ethics. As long as a team is making an ethical argument, they are doing what is expected of them.

If a team chooses to use an ethical theory in support of its position, the team must explain the theory to the judges. There is no expectation that Ethics Bowl judges are professional philosophers, nor is there an expectation that they have any familiarity with particular ethical theories. It is incumbent upon the teams who choose to use ethical theory to make it clear what the theory holds and precisely how it applies in the Ethics Bowl case under consideration. Under no circumstances should teams just be dropping names.

Again, we don't want to commit any appeals to authority. Moreover, once a team employs a particular theory in support of a position, they are on the hook for that theory, meaning that they had better know the theory well and be prepared to defend other aspects of the theory, should they pose problems for the team's position.

ADVANTAGES AND DISADVANTAGES

Even if a team chooses to never use ethical theory in support of a position, they have good reason for knowing the ins and outs of the main theories (e.g., virtue theory, consequentialism, deontology, care ethics, social contract theory, natural law theory, etc.), namely, that the teams they will be competing against will likely employ some of these theories. Moreover, judges may ask the teams about the theories, even if the teams don't bring them up during their presentation. (One of my favorite judge questions was posed by a judge sitting next to me on a panel who asked, "What do you think Aristotle's perfectly virtuous person would do in this instance?") Some teams will employ not so well-known ethical theories in hopes of tripping up their opponents. The more theory one knows, the better position one is in to guard against these sorts of shenanigans (although this strategy is not exactly in the spirit of the Ethics Bowl, and one would hope teams would refrain from employing it).

Another reason for using ethical theories in support of a position is that ethical theories can provide an opportunity to get creative. Teams employing ethical theories are not required to use them precisely as they are expressed by the great ethicists. For example, John Rawls's original position thought experiment is designed to demonstrate the correct principles of justice for a fair society. Frequently, savvy teams will use the original position thought experiment to demonstrate that some particular policy or proposal is fair, or perhaps is not fair. This seems like a completely legitimate use of Rawls's argument.

There are a few potentially serious downsides to using ethical theory to support a position in an Ethics Bowl match. First, a number of judges have an adverse reaction to teams using ethical theory. I've heard more than one judge say something to the effect of, "You used Kant to support your view, but

Kant's theory has been shown to be false." Use of particular ethical theories might be frowned on by judges who either don't like that particular theory or by judges who don't like ethical theory at all—some judges hold that all the major ethical theories are fatally flawed. Judges are admonished to not penalize teams just because they disagree with the team's position, but it is harder to make that admonishment stick if they don't like the team's reasons for holding their view.

Second, there are a number of judges who don't have a disdain, per se, for ethical theories but aren't all that excited about them either. These judges tend to think that use of ethical theory is a way to avoid digging deeper into the issues in the case. On this view, ethical theories provide crude instruments that the particulars of the case are forced into compatibility with. Support for this derives from a somewhat widely held belief that rarely in life are ethical theories perfect for sorting out tough ethical issues, so when employed in Ethics Bowl competitions, they don't warrant the highest scores.

A final concern about use of ethical theories involves their application. Many teams will attempt to get a number of ethical theories to support their position simultaneously—sort of a strength-in-numbers approach. They might argue that their position is correct because deontology, virtue theory, and consequentialism all support their proposed strategy for resolving the ethical issue. This is fine when the theories actually do that, but most of the time, they don't. These theories are frequently at odds with one another, and many Ethics Bowl cases are designed to take advantage of that fact. For example, cases will often pit the good consequences of some particular policy against the violations of some person's or group's autonomy or rights. Thus, taking the proverbial "all roads lead to Rome" approach in an Ethics Bowl competition can lead to disaster.

BALANCING RESEARCH AND THEORY

Both outside research and ethical theory play an important role in preparing for an Ethics Bowl competition, and any team that neglects one or the other does so at their own peril. That said, use of either is no simple matter, and as teams prepare for competition, they should think long and hard about how they plan on employing both, as a nuanced touch is the key to Ethics Bowl success. A further thought to keep in mind with respect to research and theory about is the value of Ethics Bowl. What does one hope to gain from the Ethics Bowl experience? The right answer to this question should also play a role in determining an approach to employing these useful tools.

* * *

Ethics Bowl was my first introduction to civics, law, politics, international relations, environmental issues, public health policy, bioethics, human rights, anthropology, and a slew of other relevant subjects that affect our world. The time I spent working toward the Bowl taught me how to research and prepare arguments; critically think and digest complex issues; conduct mature civil discourse; disagree with others while understanding and respecting their viewpoints; reflect on the world around me; evaluate my own professional and life goals; and realize the duties and responsibilities of being a member of a society, a family, and a global community. Not a day goes by where I do not pull from the lessons and thought processes learned during my time on an ethics team. This was an opportunity that I wish every student had the chance to participate in.

—Marco Antonio Cunha, High School Ethics Bowl alumnus

PART II

Best Practices

Chapter 4

Values in Ethics Bowl Design

Jeanine DeLay

Football rewards deceit—feints, off-side kicks, faked passes; Ethics Bowl rewards the pursuit of truth. Every game has values baked into its structure. What values are baked into Ethics Bowl? What are the expectations of moderators, judges, coaches, and team members? In this chapter, Jeanine DeLay, organizer of the Michigan Regional High School Ethics Bowl, analyzes and critiques Ethics Bowl as a game qua game and suggests that it is up to all of us in the Ethics Bowl community to keep innovating, to keep the Bowl vibrant, and to "live up to our values and claims for justice, and fulfill the story of an inclusive, vibrant, and flourishing community of young philosophers and ethicists."

* * *

The introduction of the Ethics Bowl academic movement in U.S. and Canadian secondary schools offers organizers and advocates a unique opportunity to ask fundamental questions about the Bowl's design and direction as it evolves. These questions appeal to philosophy educators because they are also exercises in ethical thinking.

The 2020–2022 pandemic forced Ethics Bowl organizers to address these questions head-on. We had to improvise: the Bowl could not take place in person as it had since its inception. Shifting to a virtual context seemed to emphasize those aspects of the Bowl that seemed most "game-like." We then had to consider what the Bowl really is and who it is for.

GAME DESIGN AND VALUES

Games can be defined as sequestered and artificially constructed worlds in which player choices and interactions are intentionally limited by the rules of and in the game.

Games also have values built into their very design. The Ethics Bowl is a game whose distinguishing game elements have built-in ethical values. These values are embodied in its goals, constitutive rules, and what makes it recognizable as an Ethics Bowl in contrast to a Football Bowl.

For example, a value intrinsic to the game of football is deception. This defining value is aligned with established rules that allow for fake punts, feints, and disguised plays. In Ethics Bowl, a defining value is truthfulness. Participants' presentations, commentary, and judges' questions are focused on reasoning about what is factual and true about a particular case. Lying and deceit are outside the defining rules of the game.

Hosting a virtual Bowl led us to consider how other virtual games are developed, what values are identified and emphasized, and how to focus on these values. Toward that end, we studied and discussed the work and experiences of a group of digital game designers affiliated with the Values at Play Project.[1] We undertook this reevaluation of Ethics Bowl as game to explore new ways to evaluate the Bowl and to invite different viewpoints about these ideas.

If we identify and describe the values in Ethics Bowl design, we can better understand how they combine with specific game elements to create an ethical universe. Further, we can appreciate how Bowl design conveys ethical meanings and potentially imparts values to those experiencing the game. Using the Values at Play design framework, we focused on describing four Ethics Bowl game elements and their accompanying values: (1) venue and equipment, (2) narratives, (3) reward structure, and (4) goals.

BOWL VENUE AND EQUIPMENT VALUES

Let's begin with the Bowl's fundamentals: the venue and space selected for the Bowl and its artifacts, meaning the equipment necessary to participate in and to "play the game."

Most often, the venue is a reconfigured classroom. Neither the Bowl nor team practice sessions requires a special facility. This repurposing of "academic space" in itself communicates an essential value of the Bowl: open access without the pay-to-play venue requirements that can limit participation in other high school games. Further, the fact there is no dais or stage signals that judges and students are on the same level—students all—and demonstrates intellectual humility, the notion that "we are all in this together."

The Bowl's artifacts can be separated into two categories, the first of which is low-cost pen and paper. Relying on these "knowledge objects"—rather than the digital technologies ubiquitous in our lives—reinforces the value of equitable access. Using pen and paper also signifies allegiance to traditional knowledge culture and exemplifies simplicity, evoking the reed pens and parchment that scribes in Egypt, Greece, and Rome relied on to preserve what they knew about the world. In short, Ethics Bowl declares that access to technology is not a prerequisite to think or to examine ethical quandaries together.

Nevertheless, precisely because Ethics Bowl takes place in school and relies on equipment deemed "scholarly," some students may assume they cannot join or belong to an Ethics Bowl program. In high schools everywhere, diverse groups, communities, and cultures possess unequal power, prestige, and influence. Students who do not perceive themselves as scholars may view the venue and equipment of the Ethics Bowl community as selective, unfriendly, or even hostile.

There are other economic and social barriers that limit access to, discourage, or prevent some students from participating in extracurricular activities such as Ethics Bowl. These realities, though they affect Ethics Bowl, are societal and outside the control of organizers. We can, however, continuously work on the Bowl design to be an inclusive community that draws students in rather than keeps them out.

The second category of artifacts is the case studies, which students read and analyze to prepare for the Bowl. These cases are drawn from real-world ethical dilemmas, that is, from experiences we encounter in our communities and in our daily professional and personal lives. Relying on case studies reinforces the notion that philosophy and ethics *are* essential to our education, work, and to live amicably together. They help counter the common misconception that studying philosophy and ethics are impractical and pointless pursuits in a world where economic values hold the most currency for career advancement and in the job market.

For the inaugural Michigan Bowl in 2014, we decided real-world cases needed real-world writers. Toward this end, we created the Community Case Writers. Every year, we invite residents or individuals with Michigan affiliations to write the case studies featured in the Bowl.

Our abiding idea is that home-grown case writing is one way organizers can establish an inclusive community of ethics enthusiasts from all backgrounds, age groups, identities, and life experiences. We want to convey a clear message to students, teachers, and potential writers that we are trying our best to assemble the Bowl to look like our communities. We are committed to telling everyone's ethics stories. It's one of our core values: everyone can be an ethicist and join the Bowl community.

NARRATIVE VALUES

Values are implicit in the design of any game, Ethics Bowl included. Overall, games depict and express distributive justice. This refers to the way the game distributes benefits and burdens, and whether it does so even-handedly, fairly—and justly. For example, the constitutive rules of a particular game can benefit some players over others. Basketball and volleyball tend to benefit tall players. Pro bicycling and gymnastics advantage athletes with smaller physiques. The Bowl is partial to participants with capacities for speech, hearing, and communication.

SYMMETRY: LEVELING THE PLAYING FIELD

Another value implicit in games concerns symmetry. The goal is to achieve fairness, a "level playing field." A game's symmetry ensures equal application of game rules to all teams and players. However, as we know, schools that send teams to regional Ethics Bowls exist in communities where the availability and distribution of resources—economic and political capital—vary widely and inequitably. If we prize equity in resources and are serious about defining rules that increase symmetry or the fairness the game itself, then proactive, labor-intensive, and additional measures must be taken to "level the playing field" *outside* the field. That is, we need to strive to provide equitable resources and opportunities for all participants to practice and prepare for the Bowl.

To design a fair game outside the game itself, we have had ardent and dedicated allies in our Community-Campus Partnership with the University of Michigan Department of Philosophy Outreach and the teachers/advisers at Michigan Bowl high schools. Together, we have established the Philosopher Coach Initiative. Every fall, Bowl teachers/advisers and school teams work with graduate student philosopher coaches. The Initiative relies on each partner's respective expertise. Teachers/advisers are experienced and five-star educators. Philosopher coaches know the subject and are role models for students learning about philosophy careers. Organizers are recruiters and ambassadors, striving to expand opportunities and broaden the Bowl community.

Unequal childhoods and unequal education opportunities shadow the Bowl. The Community Case Writers, Philosopher Coach Initiative, and the

Community-Campus Partnership are examples of actions we can take to try and rewrite this unequal narrative and redraw the Bowl design.

REFEREED GAME: THE ROLE OF THE MODERATOR

Procedural justice is the most recognized and analyzed value in most games, including the Bowl. It refers to the way the game proceeds and is practiced, and is distinguished by the regulative rules all players must follow—"the rules in the game." We consider game procedures just and fair when rules are applied equally to all teams and players, and when no team receives special treatment.

In most games, the regulative rules, and thus procedural justice, are adjudicated and enforced by a referee. For the Bowl, the referee is the moderator, charged with enforcing the rules fairly and justly. Bowl moderators not only manage the rounds and participants but also apply the prescriptive and mandatory game rules such as determining which team goes first and when a team's time is up.

At the Michigan Bowl, we think the role of the impartial moderator is so important that a dedicated trainer hosts a discussion about the Bowl's regulative rules and fair and just practices with new and veteran moderators every year.

RULING THE GAME: THE ROLE OF THE JUDGE

Judges have the most influence and power in the Bowl. Their votes decide which teams move on after opening rounds, and ultimately, which team wins. Complaints about the Bowl, and implicitly its design, mostly converge on judges' decisions. Like the Bowl moderators, judges are obligated to be procedurally just and fair in their scoring decisions. Judge training, education, communications, and feedback always emphasize and reiterate these responsibilities. Even so, the inclusion of judges in the Bowl's design produces the bane of all judged games: the problem of bias.

There are several ways to examine possible biases that unravel judges' intentions to make a judgment that is also procedurally just and fair in Bowl scoring. One approach is to look at bias research in judged games that can apply to the Bowl's design.[2] For example, judges may rely on *order bias,* a reluctance to assign high scores for arguments in the early rounds, because they expect to hear better-reasoned arguments in later rounds. *Reputation bias* may also be at work: this refers to a scenario in which judges assign higher scores to teams from schools known to have done well in earlier rounds or in previous Ethics Bowls.

Try as we might to prepare all our volunteers involved in the Bowl for their roles, we know that tensions exist when human decisions and judgments are built into game design.

BOWL REWARD STRUCTURE AND VALUES

We also acknowledge that game rules can be dishonored, broken intentionally, or accidentally misunderstood. When this happens, we turn to the concept of compensatory justice to reboot the Bowl—to restore symmetry and fair play.

Compensatory justice rules reward teams and players denied fair play because of procedural rules violations by other teams and players. Rewarding a penalty to the dishonored team or player is a common example.

In the Bowl, the main purpose of a compensatory rule should be to admonish and remind the offenders that they cannot break the rules they have agreed to follow without accepting responsibility and facing consequences. Any team denied fair play should be awarded a formal opportunity to offset the violation and be *compensated*, which publicly reiterates the game's aim to be procedurally just and fair.

Compensatory justice rules are not formally identified in the Bowl's design. Nonetheless, it is important to think about rules already in place that *may* be compensatory or that serve the same purpose—to offset possible infractions. One that comes to mind is points in Bowl scoring intended to keep teams attentive to a central Bowl principle: respectful dialogue.

Judges can award up to five points to each team in a section on the score sheet entitled "Respectful Dialogue." In the experience of the Michigan Bowl, judges are complaisant and easygoing in allocating these points. In most rounds, judges award five points to *both* teams. There are occasions, however, when judges will assign fewer than five points to one team, indicating that they think a team has been disrespectful. If only one team loses points in this category, this loss of points is in effect a penalty and has the *potential* to be compensatory to the team that judges scored as maximally respectful.

That said, this compensatory potential is squandered because respectful dialogue point deductions are not publicly announced by judges at the time when they occur. There is no offsetting rule that openly signals to judges and to teams that respectful dialogue points must be scored as deliberately as those given to teams for their arguments and questions. Teams neither know nor are given reasons for such deductions until they see the score sheets after all the rounds are over. Both teams are, therefore, left wondering what respectful dialogue actually means.

We are also left wondering why respectful dialogue is *scored*. On one hand, separating respectful dialogue for points indicates that it is both a value and essential to the Bowl. This is critical learning for all participants. On the other hand, student teams are the *only* participants scored on respectful dialogue. We need to collectively discuss and determine what respectful dialogue *is* and decide what it *is not* so that we can expand its current definition beyond the perfunctory nod to respect that most teams offer to judges and the other team—"Thank you for making a good point."

Scrutinizing the Bowl's design to identify the true and meaningful role of respectful dialogue will enable us to become more compelling advocates for what the Bowl stands for and stands by.

BOWL REWARD STRUCTURE: BENEFITS AND GOODS

In many ways, the absence of compensatory rules in the Bowl's design is a value and a virtue. It signals the Bowl's commitment to evolving and rewarding procedural justice and fairness rules without calling for formal rules to discipline intentional or accidental team infractions.

It is also invaluable and beneficial that the Bowl is not zero-sum. A zero-sum game is one where the winner secures the rewards at the expense of the other competitors known as the "losers." In such games, the benefits gained are fixed, limited, and scarce. The outcome of a zero-sum game is that "winners take all" and "losers" leave the game without *any* benefits.

The Bowl, however, is designed to award benefits that are shared and cumulative. *All* participants stand to gain. One team's win does not take away the Bowl's common goods: love of knowledge, reflective practice, and new reasoning skills. These intellectual values are available to everyone. Moreover, the capacity of these values to be inclusive coincides with other key values that have the same capacity, among them respect and justice. That everyone has a stake in the game and no one leaves the game without a benefit or its common goods are worthy and admirable features of Bowl design. Further, these very features are most likely to create and sustain a flourishing ethics community.

BOWL GOALS AND VALUES

If we assume one of the primary goals of Ethics Bowl is to establish a community of philosophers and ethicists in secondary schools, how can organizers spark and support this goal?

One useful way is to follow the example of the game designers at Values at Play. They identify a value-oriented game goal they wish to alter or introduce and then change an element of the existing game to observe whether it advances or inhibits this goal.

For example, we have observed that teams not advancing to next rounds tend to leave the event. These early exits show that we need to reevaluate the way we present the Bowl as an unparalleled opportunity to learn and deliberate about ethical issues at a public gathering. That is, we need to think of ways to promote the game goal of community building.

We could, for instance, develop affiliated activities to enhance camaraderie and spectacle. In the Michigan Bowl, we sponsor a Best Team Name prize and, recently, a Team Theme Song contest. Team names and songs are unconventional and reveal students' understanding that philosophy is both serious and fun. In the future, Ethics Bowl might include other activities beyond those that combine high expectations and belonging to a community with a larger vision. For example, students could create poster tutorials illustrating ethical dilemmas important to them.

Organizers could support student-curated, ethics-themed art or photography exhibits that express ideas about friendship or even differing notions of respectful dialogue. Likewise, school teams could develop and present a new Bowl convention, rule, or norm that addresses the value of what it means to belong to a school team, an organization, and to a community.

By enriching the Bowl design as a celebration and democratic gathering, we may be able to create new ways to invent a community festival that honors and recognizes the vitality of philosophy and ethics education.

We believe it is up to organizers to design a better Bowl whose goals at game's end live up to our values and claims for justice and fulfill the story of an inclusive, vibrant, and flourishing community of young philosophers and ethicists.

* * *

What makes Ethics Bowl unique is that it asks students to deal with the complexity of life and ethical decisions in scenarios where most people would want to give up trying to find the ideal decision. Ethics Bowl has taught me that it is incredibly difficult to think through certain decisions but more importantly that it is crucial for people to understand how to make ethical decisions. There also is a value in understanding other people and understanding why they might make certain decisions. This goal really manifests itself in the way that Ethics Bowl is formatted. The goal isn't to try and tear down the other team's argument in order to make your argument seem superior, but to work together toward a deeper understanding of the truth. This kind of critical thinking and respectful dialogue is becoming increasingly rare in our society, but Ethics Bowl is training students like me to challenge ourselves and to make our lives focused on intentionality and ethical behavior.

—Bobby Reuter, High School Ethics Bowler

Chapter 5

The Enduring Rewards of Ethics Bowl Case Writing

Peggy Connolly

Ethics Bowl case writing may look easy—after all, ethical dilemmas abound in media old and new and in life. But recognizing one and successfully translating it into a case that will work in Ethics Bowl is no easy job, as Peggy Connolly—veteran chair of the Intercollegiate Ethics Bowl case-writing committee—explains. Even after an ethically problematic situation is selected, it has to be written up with sufficient nuance and balance for teams to wring the most value out of the ensuing discussion. Case writers need a philosophic frame of mind to see which situations have an ethical dilemma at their core and how many details are just enough required for balance. Difficult as it is, writing cases has its own rewards. Perhaps the best cases are those sparking discussions that the writers never imagined.

* * *

"Rightly to aim in all these cases is the wise man's task."—Epictetus, *Discourses*

We all face situations in which we must act, yet we can't immediately discern what response will be the wisest and most just. Case studies can provide a road map. When we ponder case studies, we develop the ability to make credible judgments. This approach doesn't provide definitive answers to particular problems, but it hones our ability to analyze perplexing dilemmas and identify possible resolutions.

Learning about difficult situations through the lens of case studies helps humanize ethical dilemmas. This method focuses attention not only on the issues at stake but on the people involved: who gains, and who doesn't. By discussing and analyzing case studies, we learn to analyze complexities and reflect on multiple perspectives, strengthening our ability to respond to difficult situations appropriately. Ethics Bowl case discussions cultivate thoughtful deliberation of ethical dilemmas and encourage us to come up with solutions that are practical, fair, and relevant to daily life.

What variables contribute to lively discussion, complex dilemmas, rich analyses, and deepening understanding of ethical conundrums? In short, how do we write good Ethics Bowl cases?

I've thought deeply about these questions. For eighteen years, I was a case writer for the Intercollegiate Ethics Bowl, chairing the case-writing committee for ten years. During that time, five of us would meet for a week at the home of one of the committee members. We immersed ourselves in suggesting, selecting, analyzing, and editing each case in great detail. We then mercilessly perused cases for weaknesses. Based on this work, and after countless hours of discussion with colleagues, I have a good sense of what factors contribute to strong cases and what pitfalls to avoid.

Ethics Bowl cases are different than case studies used in other disciplines. Business case studies identify factors that contribute to corporate failures or successes. Marketing case studies demonstrate product effectiveness. Medical case studies examine complex medical conditions so practitioners encountering similar challenges may provide effective treatment. Jurisprudence case studies analyze legal opinions to help students master legal theory and learn to apply it to future cases.

By contrast, Ethics Bowl cases don't provide exemplars, or reveal unassailable solutions to ethical quandaries. They are designed to engender respectful, substantive discussions on challenging ethical quandaries.

TYPES OF ETHICS BOWL CASES

Not all ethical dilemmas can be translated into good Ethics Bowl cases. Ethics cases fall into two categories: those that are definitive or ambiguous.

Definitive Cases

Definitive case studies consider a particular person, action, system, or practice that is either ethically exemplary or fundamentally unethical. These cases can use positive examples of people or organizations that take an ethical stand (the Underground Railroad; Erin Brockovich, who courageously uncovered the source of water contamination that was causing serious birth defects in Hinkley, California) or negative examples of genocide, sex trafficking, fraud, or ethnic and racial cleansing. Definitive case studies are effective in analyzing factors that create ethically responsible or ethically repugnant situations. They do not, however, make effective Ethics Bowl cases, as they offer no morally compelling opposing position.

Ambiguous Cases

In comparison, ambiguous case studies do not suggest an ethically preferable option. For example, is it ethical for hackers to breach systems to expose security deficiencies? Is it ethically justifiable to discriminate against a particular group because of deeply held religious beliefs? Do parents have the right to select embryos for traits, such as deafness, that deny a benefit while providing other desirable assets, such as inclusion in a nurturing community? Good Ethics Bowl cases are, by nature, ambiguous. They provide excellent opportunities to analyze situations in which (1) multiple stakeholders have equally compelling yet competing interests, (2) there are no clear solutions, (3) no option will satisfy all parties, and (4) no matter what course of action is taken, both desirable and harmful consequences result.

ELEMENTS OF STRONG CASES AND WEAK CASES

The strongest Ethics Bowl cases include a combination of five factors (although not all are necessary for each case). They offer:

1. Multiple stakeholders with mutually exclusive interests and equally compelling perspectives
2. Nuanced issues that contain subtle complications: in other words, what appears at first glance to be simple proves more complicated after deeper analysis
3. An opportunity to discuss multiple questions or multiple approaches to analysis
4. Mutually exclusive choices
5. An engaging, riveting story

Let's consider these factors more closely.

Equally compelling perspectives—the "Other Side." The single most important factor in case writing is fully developing equally powerful arguments for each perspective of a dilemma; otherwise, there is little potential for rich discussion. Writers tend to select concerns about which they have strong feelings, particularly if they have been personally touched by the matter. This can be a strength: personally compelling experiences beget cases that are stimulating and provocative. When personal experiences or emotions are involved, however, it can be difficult to present the issue without bias that often goes unrecognized by the case writer.

Case writers also need to steer clear of cases for which there is little ethical justification for an opposing perspective. For example, it's hard to conceive of equally ethically persuasive rationales both for and against redlining, a practice that perpetuates racial, ethnic, and economic discrimination in housing.

Nuanced issues. A case about the decision to withdraw life support may appear to be simple. Consider this one: Following a sudden heart attack, an elderly parent is dying. An adult child present at the hospital states that the parent does not want extraordinary measures to prolong life but asks that life support be maintained another day until a sibling arrives. However, the second sibling claims that the parent insisted on all measures to preserve life.

Clearly, besides evoking the controversy of ending or maintaining life support, this case raises issues of prolonging life or prolonging death, autonomy, consent, and who should make end of life decisions for a person no longer capable of making choices. Nuanced stories cultivate rich analyses.

Multiple questions or approaches to analysis. Dilemmas that raise multiple questions add vigor to Ethics Bowl preparation and discussion. As teams prepare cases, they envision all the ways they—as well as the other team—could approach the topic. Consider this scenario: As cities grow and hard surfaces expand, flooding increases, which in turn endangers people and property, inflicting economic pain. Rerouting a river's course alleviates harm to cities but has enormous consequences for farmers and small communities downstream whose livelihoods and lifestyles are destroyed. Should harm to many outweigh the benefit to few? Should historical benefits have preference over current needs? Are the ethical issues raised affected by the fact that downstream communities have been historically disadvantaged? Are the consequences of disrupting ecosystems for human convenience ethically justifiable?

Mutually exclusive choices. Cases that present dilemmas in which a decision must be made that will benefit one stakeholder at the expense of another encourage vigorous dialogue. For example, suppose a couple decides to create and freeze embryos because one partner will become infertile after cancer treatment. A few years later, after a divorce and remarriage for both, the infertile spouse wants to use an embryo to have a child. The original partner refuses, no longer wanting to be a parent. Is it ethically justifiable to deny the former spouse the only option to have a biological child? Is it ethical to force parenthood on someone?

Compelling stories. Fairy tales, parables, fables, poems, histories, novels, and personal nonfictional accounts often depict regular people grappling with ethical dilemmas. Relying on these narratives when writing cases allows Ethics Bowl participants to put themselves in someone else's shoes. Discussing the case becomes a viscerally immersive experience. This helps humanize the case, that is, to consider it in its human rather than theoretical terms.

If the facts of the case include real and identifiable people, it's wise to include only verifiable public information. If facts are generic, use first names only or pseudonyms, thus avoiding inadvertently damaging someone's reputation. Another technique is to signal that the characters are fictitious by using fanciful names: Mrs. Sippi, Ida Ho, Della Ware, and Ken Tuckie.

What factors weaken cases? In general, weak cases:

1. Have critical aspects that are principally legalistic
2. Focus on polarizing issues such as abortion or partisan politics
3. Require technical, scientific, or other specialized knowledge
4. Contain critical information that can't be verified
5. Indicate the writer's commitment to a particular outcome

Let's examine in greater detail the elements that weaken cases.

Legalistic cases. Ethics Bowl cases are about ethics, not the law. For example, mineral rights give ownership to underground resources; surface rights give ownership to the land above. Often these rights are sold separately: a farmer may own the surface rights, but an oil company owns the mineral rights. If the company drills a well, the farmer is unable to farm. If the farmer prevents the oil company from drilling, the company is denied access to its rightful resources. This conundrum may seem to be a stimulating Ethics Bowl case because the parties have equal but mutually exclusive claims. However, the issues involved are heavily legalistic, rendering it inappropriate as an Ethics Bowl case.

Polarizing cases. Because well-intentioned people hold diametrically opposing views on ethical issues, respectful dialogue is essential in a civil society. A goal of the Ethics Bowl is to create an environment in which reasonable people can respectfully discuss these topics. Including cases in an Ethics Bowl on extremely polarizing topics, on which participants may hold deep personal or religious convictions, however, is counterproductive. It can lead to disruptive rather than constructive dialogue and leave a wake of unintended consequences.

When preparing for an Ethics Bowl, teams need to reach a position by consensus. If the case at hand is polarizing, those team members in the minority may feel denigrated if their values are disregarded when considering the team position. Consider this ethical dilemma: although research using embryonic stem cells has promising results for treating serious medical conditions such as Parkinson's disease and spinal cord injuries, some people consider the destruction of human embryos unequivocally unethical. Strong convictions on both sides generate strong emotions that can undermine the logic or persuasiveness of a team's position. It is important to create dialogue around inordinately controversial topics, but the Ethics Bowl is not the right venue. Divisive cases encourage diatribes, not dialogue.

Technical cases. Case writers may be tempted to construct cases that show (off) their expertise. In doing so, they forget that the focus of Ethics Bowl is the quality of the teams' presentations, not the erudition of the case writers. The Ethics Bowl gives people with limited training in ethics or philosophy the tools to address ethical challenges they may encounter in their personal or professional lives. A case on hacking may resonate with some students, but if its analysis depends on sophisticated knowledge of programming, it is not a reasonable topic for most students who participate in Ethics Bowls.

Unverifiable information. If information critical to a case is unverifiable, the case is open to ambiguous or erroneous interpretation. The key word here is "critical." Without adequate information, teams may interpret details differently and prepare cases based on disparate assumptions about fundamentals. Authentic dialogue is improbable if it is impossible to agree on the facts.

That said, not all cases are based on verifiable facts: some spring from the fertile imaginations of case writers.

Biased cases. As discussed above, compelling issues often work well as Ethics Bowl cases—except when the issue is so compelling for the writer that it reveals bias. A case writer may have a powerful urge to write an exposé of a harm suffered personally, for example, or to promote a particular cause. Resist! It is almost impossible to write a case that is not biased toward a particular ethical outcome if the writer believes to have been similarly wronged or is passionate about advancing a particular agenda. In these cases, it's too hard to see the other side of an issue clearly and fairly.

SOURCES OF INSPIRATION

Sources for Ethics Bowl cases abound. The news is full of intriguing issues that inspired many Ethics Bowl cases. Here are just a few examples of Ethics Bowl cases from the news:

- The discovery of the body of a newborn prompted the Storm Lake, Iowa, sheriff's department to subpoena the medical records of all women who

had been pregnant during the previous nine months, threatening prosecution if proof of a live baby or miscarriage was not provided.
- Ryoei Saito paid record prices for a Van Gogh and a Renoir, then announced that the paintings would be cremated with him when he died.
- To gather evidence to rid Spotsylvania County, Pennsylvania, of prostitution, undercover officers solicited and received sexual services.

Some cases are drawn from student life: students may be expelled for plagiarism, yet some professors assign students articles to write that are submitted for publication in only the professor's name; schools struggle to balance concern for the comfort and safety of transgendered students in restrooms against outraged parents fearful for the comfort and safety of their cisgendered children; municipalities that ban religious face coverings because of safety and equality concerns face charges of infringement of religious and personal rights.

Ordinary, everyday situations that may seem too trivial or mundane to be Ethics Bowl cases often work surprisingly well. Are the instructions on insurance cards that instruct drivers never to apologize or admit fault when they have caused an accident ethically justifiable? Is it ethical to blast a neighbor who frequently holds loud late-night parties with recordings of those parties via a directional microphone in the early morning? The writer of one successful case was inspired by an advertisement for Ivy League egg donors, another overheard a conversation in a restaurant, and yet another learned of a memo reminding doctors to ask patients being wheeled into surgery for permission to gather genetic material for research. One memorable case was inspired by a wrong number. After repeated requests to a home security service that erroneously listed his phone number were ignored, an exhausted man responded to incessant calls by telling callers he wasn't in the mood to deal with their burglary. He provided his name and the correct security service number so they could report him.

Movies and books are excellent sources of material, as long as reading the book or seeing the movie isn't necessary to prepare the case. Jodi Picoult's book *My Sister's Keeper* inspired a case on live organ donation. Controversy surrounding Kathryn Stockett's novel *The Help* sparked cases on the ethics of basing fictional characters on real people, and cultural appropriation.

The workplace also offers ethical dilemmas. The USA Patriot Act requires librarians to provide patron records to law enforcement in violation of the librarians' professional code of ethics. To some people, universities offering courses in pornography provide a valuable service by warning students of pornography's toxic impact on women; others believe that schools should not offer courses because they desensitize us to the reality of sexual predation.

Keep in mind that cases inspired by ordinary experiences can turn out particularly rich if the case writers are representative of diverse personal and professional backgrounds.

CONSTRUCTING GOOD ETHICS BOWL CASES

Five questions underlie case construction:

1. What is the central ethical conflict, and what are the ancillary issues (if any)?
2. Who are the stakeholders?
3. What is the appropriate level of detail?
4. What extent of research, if any, is required?
5. What theories, principles, or other ethical constructs are applicable?

We'll consider these questions more closely.

Ethical conflicts. Writers must be clear about the fundamental ethical dilemma(s) at the heart of the case. As writing progresses, understanding deepens. Perspectives may shift with additional research or as details are added. Sometimes a different ethical dilemma emerges as a more significant factor as the case evolves. If the central moral conflict is not recognizable, the case will be muddled and open to vague interpretations.

Stakeholders. To define the elements of ethical tension, the writer should identify each stakeholder and understand how each is affected by circumstances of the case. Some cases specify how stakeholders stand to benefit or be harmed, but generally it's preferable to allow students to reveal the consequences of possible resolutions.

Level of detail. Some cases require a great deal of detail to explain the ethical issue under consideration; other cases are potent when pithy. Successful cases include all critical facts, but avoid branching out in too many directions or delving into so many fine points that the case becomes difficult to analyze. A good case is ambiguous in terms of its ethical resolution but explicit in relevant facts. Similar levels of detail should be included for all perspectives to avoid the suggestion that one position is more significant than another.

Research. If a case is so complex that it requires team members to conduct extensive research, the subsequent preparation and discussion will focus more on fact-finding rather than on the ethical dilemmas. This is counterproductive. It's not unreasonable to expect students to do some research when preparing a case, but case writers need to remember that students are engaged in an Ethics Bowl, not a research project.

Applicable constructs. Good Ethics Bowl cases provide students with the opportunity to apply ethical reasoning, whether the student is a philosophy major or newly introduced to ethics. Participants are not required to employ formal ethical theories (although if they do, they are expected to use them appropriately), but they are expected to acknowledge ethical principles and decision-making that is relevant to the case. Cases should be written so they can be discussed within a variety of ethical contexts: formal ethical theories, guidelines such as the Principles of Biomedical Ethics, statements like the Declaration of Helsinki, professional codes of conduct, or a practical discussion of harms and benefits.

THE REWARDS OF CASE WRITING

Case writing is a challenging and rewarding experience, one that is best when communal. It's invaluable to ask other people to read the cases you have taken care to craft before finalizing them. We often become so familiar with a case we have been poring over that we overlook gaps in logic, missing information, or murky details. At the end of the week that our IEB case writing committee met, we were certain that, thanks to our collective intelligence, we had plumbed every aspect of each case. Yet it always delighted us that after all the hard work that went into writing cases, and no matter how comprehensively we had thought about each case we produced, Ethics Bowl team members always discovered deeper levels and richer insights, proposing arguments we hadn't considered and applying theories in innovative ways.

This is the most enduring reward of case writing.

* * *

I participated in Ethics Bowl for three years during high school, and I will never forget my team's weekly conversations during Ethics Bowl meetings. I loved these conversations because I was able to think critically about different current issues, such as gerrymandering, body transplants, and de-extinction, across a variety of perspectives. I truly believe this activity strengthened my ability to address and discuss views that opposed my own while remaining open-minded to new ideas. This activity allowed me to learn more from my peers through discussion than I could have ever learned by formulating my opinions on my own. Ethics Bowl has changed my perspective on what debate should look like and how we as young individuals should learn and strive toward this type of discourse to resolve issues (political or not) through empathy and perspective-taking.

—Lauren Christenson, High School Ethics Bowl alumnus

Chapter 6

Coaching

Winning Isn't Everything

Marcia A. McKelligan

How does a successful coach prepare a team for an Ethics Bowl competition? Marcia McKelligan believes that an Ethics Bowl coach is above all else a teacher, employing a range of skills to help students create a community of learners, cultivate their ethical intelligence, challenge their own prejudices, and develop a sensitivity to a range of legitimate ethical perspectives. McKelligan describes the cooperation, intentional and reflective listening, civility, and respect for the diversity of views that leads team members to grasp the ethical significance of rich existential dilemmas captured in Ethics Bowl cases. She further observes that Ethics Bowl creates an extended community of individuals (even team members' parents) who care about authentic ethical deliberation and civil discourse.

* * *

2:30 a.m. The alarm is set for 6:30. The Ethics Bowl competition is tomorrow, and sleep is elusive. The night before the event is the time that you take stock of all that your team has accomplished while preparing, all the weak spots you hope are not starkly revealed in public tomorrow. It's a time when you have sudden flashes of insight into how a particular argument might have been fixed or a certain objection rebutted. You hope that one really shaky case isn't called. "The team is only as strong as its weakest case," you've said many times.

Right now many of the students are probably still up too. They are frantically re-rewriting, or memorizing, or practicing in the mirror. Some are terrified, some eager, and some confident they are ready. (Those students are *probably sleeping.) You've checked your phone and email for the last time. No new "What if I changed my argument this way?" queries. They're settling in, and your work is done.*

Unlike sports, there's no midgame coaching: no substitutions, no play calling, no timeouts, and certainly no running about on the sidelines. Once the match is set to begin, after you take just a moment for some rousing words of encouragement—"You guys are ready! Go get 'em!"—there is nothing left for a coach to do at a match but sit quietly, with proper poker face, and watch.

How lucky can you get, to be a part of all that?

WHAT COACHES DO

There's no best way to coach a team. Some coaches may assemble the team, explain what is required, share some strategies, and then send the students off to work independently, checking in maybe once a week. At the other extreme, a coach might work regularly with the team, explain to members how each case should be understood and what positions and arguments it would be wise to put forward.

Most of us fall somewhere in the middle, meeting quite frequently with our teams but working and struggling along with them to understand and reason our way through the cases, guiding rather than directing. What coaches choose to do, and indeed, what it is appropriate to do, will depend on the level and type of school or institution, the age and background of the participants, as well as their own pedagogical preferences.

Whatever the method, at its core, Ethics Bowl coaching is a form of teaching. Coaches impart knowledge; encourage independent and critical thought; hone students' research, writing, and speaking skills; and foster teamwork. They also contribute to the personal growth of team members: one, by insisting that ethical conviction be supported by evidence and argument rather than just emotion; and two, by helping students learn to conduct themselves honorably and graciously in victory and defeat.

Recruiting a Team

A coach needs a team, and there are several ways to attract new players. Personally contacting promising students you've taught, putting out a general call, holding interest meetings, and asking friends and colleagues for recommendations all work well. Word of mouth among current and past participants is probably the most effective producer of recruits. The Ethics Bowlers themselves are the best sales assistants a coach can have. When things are going well, a coach can count on an almost continuous chain of participants as students commend the activity to younger students and they in turn later bring in new recruits.

Some coaches hold tryouts to determine who will be welcomed onto the team. Those who don't make the cut might serve as alternates or researchers. Another way to accommodate all those who would like to join is to create multiple teams, if the regional host permits more than one team from a school or the coach's institution has the resources to travel to two events.

Preparing the Team to Participate

An important first question is, "What are we trying to accomplish here?" It seems reasonable to answer that we are trying to win a competitive event, but that answer overlooks most of what makes Ethics Bowl worth the time and effort we devote to it. So it might be smarter and better to say we are hoping to prepare and execute so well that we do well, learn a lot from our work, and enjoy one another's company along the way.

We in the Ethics Bowl community like to say that an Ethics Bowl match is a respectful conversation between two teams, all of whose members are ready to speak knowledgeably and insightfully about an issue, listen carefully and charitably to the opposing team, and then respond to them respectfully and constructively. The teams are not engaged in verbal combat, they're not trying to "score points," and they would never engage in grandstanding. Rather, a good Ethics Bowl match is a model of civil discourse.

All this may be true. However, although we may call a match a discussion or a conversation, it's a conversation that somebody wins and somebody loses. The other team is the *opposing* team, and teams have to *literally score points* in order to win. The tension between the highly competitive nature of Ethics Bowl (and many of its participants) and its lofty ethical aspirations is one of the charms of the event. Of course teams and their coaches want to win. With victory come pride in accomplishment, public recognition, and often a chance to participate at the national level.

If victory were the only goal, though, most teams would be disappointed most of the time. A coach must help a team appreciate both the intrinsic value of the activity and also the rewards it brings independently of wins and losses. The chief joy and lasting value of Ethics Bowl come not from winning but from the camaraderie, intellectual challenge, and productive collaboration that are an essential part of it. Years later, we will all reminisce just as fondly about our stumbles as about our triumphs.

But winning is terrific. No one likes to lose, and the coach's job is to turn the team into a formidable contender. There is some background information teams ought to know in order to get started. It is good for teams to have a basic grasp of ethical theories such as utilitarianism, virtue ethics, or Kantianism; some well-known thought experiments such as the "trolley problem" and John Rawls's "veil of ignorance"; ethical concepts such as obligation and permissibility; and foundational ethical principles such as fairness and benevolence.

How much attention teams should give to ethical theory in an Ethics Bowl is a topic of considerable debate; it is not required that a team cite a theory or formal principle in support of an argument. The team should construct an argument in terms accessible to anyone, not just philosophers or ethics specialists; nevertheless, teams are often asked by opponents or judges to identify the "ethical framework" they are relying on. Given that the team members will have produced good ethical arguments for their view, they in fact have a framework. It's helpful to be able to name it.

Seeing the season's cases for the first time is oddly exhilarating. They will be at the center of the team's attention for months. Ethics Bowl preparation is like a class—the syllabus for which has been created by someone else. The case writers drive the course content, and their cases are our primary texts. Research provides the secondary source material.

At first reading, the case packet might seem to be just a bewildering collection of one-page essays about interesting and sometimes unfamiliar topics. To deal with them effectively, students must try to identify all the ethically relevant features of each case: what is at stake in the scenario presented; the likely outcomes if certain actions are taken or omitted; the interests, rights, and obligations of the major players; any conventions, rules, or laws that might govern the situation; the historical background and context of the issues; and so on.

This preliminary analysis is a necessary step toward discerning what issue is at the heart of the case and developing a position on it. Case analysis is a skill that takes some time to acquire, and familiarity with the tools of ethical inquiry is very useful, but close reading and clear, careful thinking are even more important. Coaches can help develop analytical and argumentative proficiency in students just as all practitioners can teach others their special skills.

The founders of Ethics Bowl had the fiendish but brilliant notion that the question that will be asked at the competition will not be included in the case packet. A look at past cases reveals that most often they are merely fairly straightforward factual descriptions of events or situations along with some reaction and commentary from knowledgeable or concerned sources—something like this (tongue firmly in cheek here):

> Betty Lou got a new pair of shoes. She wore them out of the store, but on the way home, she tripped and injured her knee on the loose, uneven bricks of the

sidewalk. Customers report a brief altercation between Betty Lou and the proprietor of the store and speculate that she might have been upset when she left. Her mother said it was Betty Lou's fault for wearing those cheap sweatshop shoes, but her friends say the sidewalk should have been in better shape and are petitioning the City Council to make the needed repairs. Speaking for his client, attorney Robert Freeman says the shoe store is not responsible for selling Betty Lou ill-fitting shoes. (https://www.youtube.com/watch?v=-8A3K_Lppe8)

Looking at this case, we would wonder what the question might be. Is this a case about personal injury liability? Seems that way. But maybe the issue is personal responsibility. Family relationships could be relevant here: Betty Lou's mother does not seem supportive. Why not? Perhaps the main concern in the case is our hyperlitigious society. Or maybe the case points us to problems with "fast fashion."

Teams spend considerable time attempting to discern what the focus of the case is in order to be ready for "the question." The cases themselves are so remarkably rich with ethically interesting possibilities that the teams will inevitably consider multiple questions. In the Betty Lou case, we'd talk about all the questions noted above. Team brainstorming may be the best way to unearth all the possibilities in a given case. The coach can prod and guide and contribute ideas as well.

Once the team has tentatively settled on the main issues and begins to formulate and discuss possible positions and the arguments for them, the coach should encourage the students to offer criticism of what their teammates say. Students are often reluctant to be perceived as challenging one another, but it is essential for an honest and clear-headed understanding of the cases that they do so. The only way a student's presentation can improve is for it to be energetically questioned and criticized.

The coach can show how to object respectfully by actively participating in the conversation and politely raising competing points, asking frequently, "What would you say if . . . " The coach can help create an atmosphere of trust between members rather than one of insecurity or defensiveness. Similarly, the coach can explicitly welcome the expression of a wide range of viewpoints. No one should be pressured into changing their stance on a case if they can argue effectively for it. The goal is to present a well-considered and defensible position, not one that everyone will find agreeable.

By midseason or even earlier, it's good to stage a mock competition, either by finding colleagues or students to serve as the opposing team or by dividing the team itself into two smaller groups. If the institution is fielding two teams, then they can square off against one another. Zoom and other platforms allow us to scrimmage virtually with teams from distant schools.

One purpose of this exercise is to fire up team members' critical-thinking cylinders to make sure they are considering all relevant points. In addition, bringing in outsiders can help dislodge a team that's wedged into a constricted line of thinking about a case. For first-timers, the mock competition alerts them that presenting and responding to a case are much harder than they had expected. For veterans, a public airing of their position can lead them to realize it needs more work.

THE EVENT

Although team readiness is unlikely to improve once the Ethics Bowl is underway, the big event still offers opportunities for learning and personal growth on the part of both coaches and team members. During the matches, the coaches, who in spite of themselves are often now totally invested in the outcome, must avoid even an encouraging nod to their team. Passively watching can be agonizing. Sometimes, when students have put in a performance of expectation-defying greatness, we could weep with pride and gratitude. (Once or twice we have done that very thing.)

More typically, from the comfortable and clear-headed position of a spectator, we hear every mistake our team makes and note every missed opportunity. When a judge asks a question that the team should be able to answer with ease and they request time to confer, then emerge looking befuddled, we must sit there helplessly. These events develop our patience and self-control while chipping away helpfully at our illusion of control over our teams' performance.

A defeat at a Bowl provides a unique opportunity for a coach to help the team cope with a loss. Like many bad impulses, it's shockingly tempting to tell the disappointed team it's not their fault they lost—it was carelessness or inept judging. But instead, of course, we should say that although we disagree with the judges, we should have confidence in their integrity and conscientiousness. We can acknowledge the limitations of our own judgment in this situation and try to determine what the judges may have seen in our performance that was subpar. We can also note that judging is extremely difficult. (To verify that, every coach should serve as a judge at some point.) The conventional condolence that "you win some, you lose some" may be as keen an insight as any to share with a dejected team.

Something remarkable always happens when a team formally faces off against other schools, whether the team wins or loses. Some impassioned competitive genie is unbottled. Just like that, all participants see why they worked so hard. Emotions, positive and negative, run high. Students who said they like Ethics Bowl well enough but probably wouldn't do it again are suddenly saying they can't wait for next year. Competition is an absolutely essential part of Ethics Bowl that can bring out our best and worst qualities, so we have to use it to help our students and ourselves learn to lose with dignity—and win with humility.

After the Bowl: Looking Back and Looking Ahead

A team celebration is a must. An honest debriefing after a competition is helpful. Team members enjoy dissecting the matches, complaining about judges or other teams (a little bit is cathartic), and sharing their thoughts about what happened and what it means. The coach can say what went well and what needs improvement. If the institution has earned a bid to compete in a higher-level competition, a preliminary discussion of who should be on the team can begin. Otherwise, talk can turn to what we should do differently and better next year.

Since Winning Isn't Everything, What Else Is There?

Ethics Bowl provides a nearly incomparable educational experience for its participants. Thanks to the cases themselves and the research necessary to provide context, team members and coaches learn about many new situations and issues, often well ahead of public awareness. In the past few years, the case writers, who excel at sniffing out a good controversy from a short news piece, have led teams to acquaint themselves with such topics as geoengineering to combat climate change, the shortage of lethal execution drugs, ethical problems with autonomous cars, testosterone regulation of women Olympians, and electronic social credit systems.

More significant is the fact that Ethics Bowl demands more intellectually from students than their coursework typically does. Students report this consistently, and alumni often say that participation in Ethics Bowl was the most academically and intellectually consequential thing they did in college. Students are grateful for the extra challenge and higher standards of Ethics Bowl. Coaches contribute meaningfully to that benefit by making tough demands of their teams.

Particularly noteworthy in the current climate is that freedom of thought and expression, and appreciation of the value of diverse viewpoints is essential to the very existence of Ethics Bowl, which could not function in a monolithic, repressive, or censorious environment. The hard but honest dialogue that has to occur if teams are to gain insight into the complexities of the questions they are tackling promotes in team members an appreciation of the merits of competing points of view and fosters intellectual humility.

Coaches have an outsized influence here, in that their role requires them to lift students out of ethical and intellectual complacency. What may seem at the time as mere coach-y strategizing—"Consider the other side!"—will, one hopes, take root and become an intellectual habit that will serve our students well in school, work, and civil society.

Ethics Bowl also builds a robust and enduring sense of community that we experience in different ways. Like many other coaches, I hear regularly from former team members. Some have started teams where they are now teaching, and some of their students are coaching as graduate students. Some have traveled across the country to watch our school participate in Nationals. Parents of *former* Bowlers have come to Bowls.

Perhaps most remarkable is that Andy Cullison, former director of the Prindle Institute for Ethics at DePauw University, was a member of DePauw's very first Ethics Bowl team in 1999! An institution's "family tree" of Ethics Bowl participants would be inspiring to see. I expect we are nowhere close to reaching the full potential and value of Bob Ladenson's simple but ingenious brainchild.

* * *

> Ethics Bowl gave me a place to think in community. The event itself and all the work leading up to it fostered a space where my friends and I could grow our thoughts and pass them through the world as it is. Always fun to see what came out the other end. Ethics Bowl didn't lead me in a direct path toward my current profession, which is making vaccines. But it created space for my thoughts and the way I think to grow consistently. It is this change to the way I think that lets me choose what way I can live best now—and lets me ask and choose again tomorrow.
>
> —Akash Dagur, High School Ethics Bowl alumnus

Chapter 7

Listening Well
Judging an Ethics Bowl

Wendy C. Turgeon

Anyone can judge an Ethics Bowl, says veteran judge Wendy Turgeon, underscoring one of the most democratic features of the event. Yet no one claims the job is easy. Although a philosophical background isn't required, the best judges can listen, empathize, summarize, and question; they are flexible, reflective thinkers who know they are there to teach as well as grade. Dr. Turgeon outlines how successful judges prepare for the Bowl. She relishes the rewards and exhilaration she feels after witnessing engaged students tackle serious issues. In many ways, she concludes, "they inspire those of us who judge to think more carefully about our own ethical decision-making; they also help us to a deeper respect for these young citizens and future leaders." Not a bad reward for a day's work.

* * *

Volunteering to be a judge in an Ethics Bowl is an incredibly rewarding experience. Having judged high school Ethics Bowls for over ten years now, I can assuredly say that the experience is exhilarating and intellectually rewarding. Not only are you supporting the young people who have spent countless hours working on a range of ethics cases to present to the panel of judges, but you will strengthen your own reflective approach to confronting ethical issues.

Ethics Bowls originated in colleges but have spread to high schools and recently to middle schools. The teams are sponsored by the school but require hours of volunteer time from the coaches—often a teacher—and even more hours for the students to work on all of the cases and prepare to present them to total strangers—you. Bowls begin locally, winners going to a regional and then ultimately the national-level match. Judges are key players in the Ethics Bowl experience because they respond to the young people's weeks of preparation by listening and evaluating their work.

As a judge, you are there to offer commentary and, yes, judgment, on the quality of the reasoning presented to you during the well-scripted session. Recognize that the young people will be very nervous. Even after hours of practice, it is quite daunting for a team to face a panel of unknown judges who will measure its success analyzing a case and responding to the other team's analysis and comments. The tenor of your contribution should be thoughtful, critical in the sense of analytic, but also supportive and welcoming. Would you have had so much courage when you were thirteen, fifteen, nineteen? Perhaps not! Ideally your questions help the team articulate more clearly its own position on the issue at hand and perhaps offer an opportunity to reconsider their initial statements.

This chapter will offer guidelines on who makes a good judge, how to prepare for judging the cases, and best practices while serving as a judge on the day of the match.

WHO CAN BE A JUDGE?

Here is the good news: anyone who is willing and interested! An extensive background in philosophy is not necessary. That is not to say that some acquaintance with philosophy is not useful. If you have some familiarity with ethical theories, this can help you better respond to the team arguments. Some teams like to introduce philosophers' names and theories, but too often they do not quite get them right. Some background knowledge can help you gently probe their understanding of the implications of the categorical imperative of Immanuel Kant or Mill's greatest happiness principle.

But this background is not a requirement. Judges come from all professions: law, medicine, journalism, technology, academics from all disciplines, as well as business leaders from the local community. Retirees and college students make excellent judges, as can teachers—assuming they do not have a vested interest in the teams they judge! The main criteria are:

- An interest in preparing for the presentations and in ethical reflection
- A willingness to be objective, fair, and supportive
- An ability to listen carefully to the arguments presented
- The skill to formulate helpful questions

Preparing to Judge an Ethics Bowl—Your "Homework"

Once you commit to judging, try your best to keep the commitment. Mark the date on your calendar. The organizers will supply supporting material. You should know how to contact a point person if problems arise. Cancelling can wreak havoc for the organizers, but they realize conflicts arise. If you must cancel, please give them as much lead time as possible. However, try your best to see this commitment as an ethical promise to be there and serve.

To best prepare for the day of the bowl, read all the twelve to fifteen cases carefully in advance of the event. (Team members have access to the cases as well.) You will not know which cases you will be called upon to adjudicate, so review all of them. Many of the cases will be taken from recent news sources while others may involve more personal ethical decisions. Each year a dedicated group of volunteers crafts the cases for that year. Some will include references to laws and precedent; others may seem deceptively simple. To prepare for each case, we recommend you ask yourself the following questions and consider these suggestions:

1. What are the key ethical issues? Often there is more than one. If there are multiple ethical dimensions, does one seem more important or central to the issue at hand? Outlining each issue will help you evaluate the arguments presented by the teams during the meet.
2. Who are the "players" in this case? That is, identify the "moral agents" who must decide, act, or take a specific stand on a given issue. Are there multiple agents in the case? If so, is each faced with the same decision or perhaps a different one?
   a. There may also be "moral patients"—individuals affected by the decisions and actions of the moral agents. You will want to gauge the ways in which these moral patients may be affected by the actions of those who must do something.
   b. In some situations, a character could be both the agent and the patient. For example, someone refuses to undergo a blood transfusion or chemotherapy. In cases like these, individuals have to not only act but also make a decision that affects themselves or others. Of course, even if the decision primarily affects the agent, others might also be affected collaterally. Sorting out all the individuals involved is an important step in forming a position on the case.
3. Many Ethics Bowl cases introduce laws and legal precedent and apply them to the situation under discussion. Noting relevant laws is helpful, but remember that the goal is not to prepare a legal brief on the issue at hand. There is a difference between what is legal and what is ethical; you are not being asked to cite a law to justify an action as ethical.

This same consideration applies to religious beliefs. It may be sticky to argue that a particular religious belief is unacceptable, but that might actually be the case from the perspective of ethics. Imagine a religious sect espousing that parents have ultimate control over their children and can beat them or perhaps even kill them if they so choose. In such a dramatic case, one might argue that ethically such beliefs are unwarranted and misguided and as such should not be honored simply under the guise of religious freedom. Or perhaps that is precisely what you will want to argue. But consider this angle so as to be prepared if the presenters pick it up. As well, if a team cites a theological belief to support an action as ethical, a judge can point out that this is not a sufficient *philosophical* argument.

In short, when preparing your own analysis of a given case, it is well worth listing the relevant laws, cultural beliefs, and religious practices that seem relevant to the issue at hand.

A QUICK PRIMER ON ETHICAL THEORIES

Although judges are not required to have studied classic ethical theories, knowing the basic ideas informing each theory can help you frame your analyses of the cases. Ethics is often broadly framed in terms of moral rules grounded in outcomes/consequences or intentions. A third approach is called "Virtue or Character Ethics." Let us consider each in turn.

1. Utilitarianism, one of the major theories of contemporary ethics, defines right/wrong strictly in terms of consequences. That is, the right action maximizes happiness and/or minimizes pain compared with other possible actions. A utilitarian estimates the consequences on all involved, not just the person acting; the fact that one person is happy is not sufficient to render their action right if others are suffering more.

As you study the cases, consider the outcomes on both agents and patients. Outcomes are seldom all good or all bad, so reflect on the range of results from the possible decisions faced by the agents. What will happen to the main protagonist, if there is one? Additionally, who else might be affected by their decision and in what ways? Is there a relevant timeline that you one must take into account? If the issue is societal, many individuals may be affected; if personal ethical decisions are being considered, the outcome may be far more circumscribed.

We often rely on utilitarian reasoning when crafting laws or general guidelines. We might encounter this in terms of an argument for a position on the grounds that it is for "the greater good."

2. As we consider outcomes, we need to consider intentions. This is the main tenet of "deontological ethics" as formulated by Immanuel Kant.

Kant insisted that actions were of moral value only if done with the right intention, a very specific choice on the part of the agent to do what is right because . . . it is right.

Of course, you do not need to know a lot about Kant's theory to see that often intentions matter greatly as we try to estimate the ethical quality of an action. For example, I may donate a thousand dollars to a charitable organization, and you may see that as praiseworthy. But if you were to learn it was a court-ordered donation as part of my sentence, I suspect your view of my donation would change. The charity may not care; generally all donations are welcome. However, I no longer look like such a generous and caring individual now, do I? (We recognize that one might argue that a donation of "tainted money" should be rejected, so keep that option in mind.)

Similarly, if I accuse my coworker of sexual harassment, that is admirable . . . but what if I did so to get their job? And what if that coworker had been a good friend?—would I have turned them in? You can see that although intentions may be hard to gauge, they can matter a great deal in evaluating one's ethical values, both in terms of the quality of the agent and of the act itself. When judging a case, consider both.

3. If you evaluate the character of the people involved in a given case, you are relying on the theory of virtue or character ethics. Perhaps the case does not really raise questions about what to do but rather questions about who one is as a person. Originating in the Western tradition with Plato and Aristotle, this approach to ethics has enjoyed renewed interest and attention recently, perhaps because it often proves far more appealing and engaging than other abstract theories.

When considering a case, think how you would describe the characters involved. What good qualities (virtues) do they demonstrate? Do they exhibit bad qualities (vices)? Framing ethical analysis in terms of virtues and vices allows us to acknowledge the human element in our decisions and to consider how those decisions and actions reflect on who we are.

Clearly, some acquaintance with these classic ethical theories can be helpful, but it's far more important to carefully think through each case that might be presented and consider it from every angle. If you can anticipate possible positions offered by the teams, you will have an easier time when called upon to question and comment on the teams' performances.

THE DAY OF THE ETHICS BOWL

The judge's first task is to listen very carefully to the team presenting, the responding team, and then the presenters' response to the other team's comments and questions. Take notes; it helps. Focus directly on their arguments; these will form the basis of your questioning.

During the judges' questions portion of the round, be courteous to your fellow judges, and do not dominate the floor. Ask a question as succinctly as you can; this way, the team will have enough time to demonstrate their ability to respond. Judges are not called upon to offer their own analysis of the case or ask long-winded questions, often answering them themselves. Academics are particularly prone to this mistake, but anyone caught up in the case itself can end up doing this.

You can bring up a point you think the presenting team missed and ask them to address it, or to further develop a position that they presented. Teams should take into account arguments that may be used against the position they advocate; if they fail to do so, offer them the opportunity. For example, you might say, "You gave some good reasons for why social media should not be censored by a school, but what might be an argument to censor it?"

One tactic to avoid is asking multiple questions, one after another. This can flummox the team and lead to a poor response. As an Ethics Bowl judge, your role is to support the team by giving them the chance to refine their arguments. This sets a positive and dialogic tone to the discussion. But if there is enough time to ask a follow-up question, feel free to do so.

You will also want to gauge your question to the level of the team; a college team may have a more sophisticated approach than a middle school one. The questioning period is a time for teams to "think on the fly." Students can really shine when responding to a challenging question you pose.

SCORING

Most sessions have three judges, so do not worry that the outcome of the match rests entirely on your shoulders. When scoring the presentation, recognize that teams may prepare for the event quite differently. One team may divide up the cases so that one or two members do the heavy lifting; another team may orchestrate a response in which every member of the team contributes to their presentation. One approach is not necessarily better than another. Do not reward more points for one tactic over the other even if you prefer one. Likewise, do not reward a team that uses the names of philosophers and their theories as somehow more sophisticated or better prepared than a team that does not. Focus on what they say, not whom they quote.

And finally, Ethics Bowls are not debates. This is a very important, and often overlooked, distinction. The teams have been preparing to talk with each other, not to argue against each other. In some matches, both teams may agree on the ethical principles and actions. In this case, focus is on which team made the better presentation and took into account alternatives in their analysis. To score the responding team, ask yourself if they brought up points that the presenting team missed or did not adequately address.

After the results are announced, it is courteous to compliment both teams for their hard work and effort. Generally we do not advise commiserating with the losing team—and please, do not openly disagree with the results even if you believe the outcome was not to your liking. Stay neutral and supportive. At this point in the round, the participants, whether happy or unhappy, are thinking about their next match. Your calm and supportive demeanor will help them prepare for it.

FEEDBACK

Some Bowls build in time for judges to write short analyses for the teams to review after the event. Be as positive as you can, offering constructive suggestions, not devastating critiques. Remember that each team's performance depends to a large extent on the quality of their coaching as well as the dedication of the team members themselves. Coaches who have participated in prior Ethics Bowls become better coaches, and it often shows.

Your positive, focused feedback is welcome and can help the team improve for the following year or even for the national bowl, should the team qualify. However, if a coach or team member approaches you with questions—or even worse, challenges—it is best to explain that you will submit your feedback in writing, not in the heat of the moment. Teams and coaches are advised to not corner a judge in this way, but may well forget about Ethics Bowl etiquette in the heat of the moment.

THE REWARDS OF JUDGING

As you leave the event at the end of a long day, you may find yourself reflecting, as I do, on the pleasure you derived from meeting other judges. They come from all walks of life and share your passion for supporting young people in their quest to become good thinkers.

You will probably also find yourself impressed by the young people's level of engagement, hard work, and thoughtfulness. Many judges, myself included, leave Ethics Bowls realizing just how powerful a voice our youth have and that they deserve more opportunities to speak their minds. In many ways, they inspire those of us who judge to think more carefully about our own ethical decision-making; they also help guide us to a deeper respect for these young citizens and future leaders.

After many years of judging Ethics Bowls, I am always impressed with the careful reasoning, passion for good thinking, and dedication to values that matter. I take that learning experience with me into my own encounters with ethical issues.

Judges validate all the hard work and effort students—and their coaches—invested in preparing for the Bowl over the course of many months. You took time from your busy schedules, work and personal, to support them in their endeavors. That alone speaks volumes to the young people and their coaches. Once you have served as a judge, we think you will be eager to do it again.

* * *

Through Ethics Bowl, I acquired an appreciation for civility. No longer do I take refuge in vain ad hominem arguments. Instead, I strive to approach my conflicts from an alternate perspective. As human beings, we have a natural propensity for rational behavior. Affording us the ability to contemplate the very inlets of our mind, this proclivity—coupled with gracious contestation—fosters an environment where intellectual inclusivity may flourish. My participation in Ethics Bowl aided in this realization; through common conversation, I learned to embrace the intricate and/or diversified means of deriving objective virtue from increasingly subjective matters.

—Nicole Patricia Zacchia, High School Ethics Bowl alumnus

Chapter 8

Beyond Argument

Learning Life Skills through Ethics Bowl

Andrew Cullison

Beginning his Ethics Bowl career as a college student, Andrew Cullison now organizes and coaches high school and college teams. In his years of involvement, he has come to appreciate the event's long reach. The very skills participation in Ethics Bowl hones are those many believe are crucially important to success later in life, no matter what field one enters. Its very structure accomplishes this preparation deliberately with careful, graduated scaffolding along the way, which allows students time to realize that winning is only one aspect of Ethics Bowl they come to value. As they gain self-confidence, self-respect, and acquire public speaking and ethical leadership skills, students see that Ethics Bowl prepares them for life.

* * *

In 1999, DePauw University fielded its first team in the Intercollegiate Ethics Bowl. Participating as a member of that team is one of my most vivid college memories. The experience had such an impact that I have been actively involved in Ethics Bowl ever since. I do this because I think that Ethics Bowl is one of the best educational experiences a student can undergo. Some may think that Ethics Bowl is simply another form of debate, a way to induce students to learn to argue with others, but this couldn't be further from the truth. Ethics Bowl is the intellectual equivalent of a CrossFit exercise workout; that is, it strenuously tones the mind and soul together.

This chapter will discuss the unique ways in which Ethics Bowl cultivates five important life skills: ethical reasoning, public speaking, noncompetitive dialogue, self-confidence, and resilience. We will then discuss how these skills foster capacities we hope our children and students will develop: the strength to exhibit ethical courage and to become ethical leaders.

ETHICAL REASONING SKILLS

One of the fundamental skill sets that Ethics Bowl cultivates overlaps with the skills many educators and child development researchers identity as important to later success in life. These ethical reasoning skills have four components:

- Ethical Awareness—the ability to identify that an issue is in fact an ethical issue
- Ethical Reasoning—the ability to identify all the different positions reasonable people might take with respect to an ethical issue *and* identify all the reasons and arguments they might have for that position
- Ethical Decision-Making—the ability to weigh those reasons in a thoughtful manner to decide what to think or do about an ethical issue
- Ethical Dialogue—the ability to engage in thoughtful, deliberative conversation with other people about an ethical issue (particularly people with different backgrounds and perspectives)

Let's go through each of these skills in turn.

When teams first receive the set of regional cases, they typically go through all the scenarios and have an initial conversation about each. Their first main goal is to determine what ethical issues the cases raise. (Students aren't told in advance what ethical issues they might need to discuss; they have to spend months figuring that out for themselves.) This induces them to cultivate ethical awareness. Because this process is undertaken as a team, the group is more likely to identify key ethical issues than any single person could have done individually.

As a result, over time, students not only become more ethically aware for themselves, but also become sensitive to the fact that people think differently than they do.

The less homogeneous teams can be, the better. Ideological diversity is a huge team asset. One of the best Ethics Bowl teams we have seen had two cocaptains: one was a leader of the College Republicans, the other founded the College Democratic Socialist Club (because the College Democrats weren't "liberal enough"). The captains became great friends. We like to think that the fact that they developed their ethical awareness together, as team members, fostered their personal friendship.

Once students have identified the ethical issues, their next step is to map out all the different opinions that might be expressed in response to the ethical issues they've identified, even if the opinions are not ones each student would individually endorse. Teams need to think about each reason for and against each opinion that is raised. This process *directly* cultivates the second skill, ethical reasoning.

Next, students decide on the team's position for each case. At this phase, things can get a little tricky, and perhaps even heated, because students need to go through the motions of *deciding what to do*. However, one of the benefits of Ethics Bowl is that they make these decisions when the stakes are low; that is, they are not actually enacting decisions, but rather figuring out what steps they would take if they had to decide on a course of action.

Cultivating the skill of being able to engage in ethical dialogue is one of Ethics Bowl's major goals. To help them, students are given a detailed rubric that clearly articulates how they will be judged. This rubric is essentially a road map for how to discuss ethical quandaries with others and to be respectful and civil even when giving voice to their own strongly held convictions. Indeed, the entire event is structured so that with a bit of training, students can come together in this way.

PREPARING FOR LIFE AFTER ETHICS BOWL

Learning the above skills is important, but participating in Ethics Bowl fosters many other significant skills that overlap with the large, overarching goals we have for our students.

Public Speaking Skills

Ethics Bowl is unique in its approach to developing public speaking skills. It scaffolds the nurturing of these skills in ways that other "speaking" cocurricular activities do not. Delivering an oral argument to support an ethical position is a very difficult skill for many people, often more difficult than composing a position paper. To make the task facing Ethics Bowl participants even harder, they do not have access to PowerPoint, slide decks, or any visual aids during the actual event. As a result, Ethics Bowlers need to be very intentional when organizing and presenting positions. They need to provide clear sign-posts to judges and spectators indicating how their arguments are progressing.

As well, there are no rules about how extensively each team member must speak during any individual match. A team can organize itself so that all members speak, or only one or two. This means that students can join an Ethics Bowl team even if they are shy about public speaking. They can find their own comfort level and still participate—by helping with a team's research, taking notes during matches, or speaking up during trial prep sessions only. Students who feel a bit braver but not yet ready to argue a team's position for minutes at a time may feel comfortable introducing the team's position or summing it up, which would require less than a minute of speaking time. And students who aren't ready to speak at all may build up their courage simply by sitting in front of an audience, shoulder-to-shoulder with teammates. Other students may want to keep silent.

And perhaps, over time, shy students who are encouraged to join teams will begin to master their fears of speaking in front of groups simply by sitting in front of an audience. We've all seen students find themselves caught up in the excitement of the event and, much to their own surprise, weigh in with an insightful comment. By serving on a team immersed in spirited back-and-forth, even hesitant-to-speak-up students may start to think, "Hey, I can do this."

Few other public speaking activities allow for this kind of flexibility. In debate and similar events, students are often required to stand up and speak, by themselves, in front of spectators. For a shy student, this can feel like being tossed into the deep end of the pool and told to start swimming. Ethics Bowl, with its focus on teams, consensus building, and carefully planned structure, gives all students the opportunity to make microcontributions at first and gradually assume larger roles. Coaches and team members often help with this growth.

Approaching Dialogue Noncompetitively

Ethics Bowl doesn't simply help students become better public speakers; it helps make them *virtuous* speakers and good conversational partners. When we welcome students to Ethics Bowls at the Prindle Institute for Ethics, we emphasize this value by relating a story about Socrates and the Sophists. The Sophists were in many ways like ambulance-chasing attorneys. In fact, they were worse because they ran schools that trained the ambulance-chasing attorneys of the day. They promised to give people the ability to sue other people in court and win arguments so that they could make a fortune from lawsuits even when they knew their position was weak. They specialized in "making the weaker argument seem stronger." In fact, the word *sophistry* is a pejorative in our language because of these folks.

Socrates despised the Sophists. In his view, Sophists weaponized deliberation for individuals to use for personal gain. According to Socrates, winning arguments was not the point of dialogue. In his view, we engage in dialogue and analyze arguments to discover truth together—or to at least discover the best reasons we have for believing what we believe to be true.

Ethics Bowl builds on this understanding. Ultimately, students are scored on whether they are good conversational participants and deep ethical thinkers. Winning teams demonstrate that they have probed the ethical depths of the cases more deeply than the other team. In this way, Ethics Bowl helps students to learn how to engage in dialogue and that argument need not be combative. Instead, civil argument can provide a framework through which two competing sides can come together, probe a difficult issue, and perhaps arrive at a mutually agreeable solution. This, in turn, broadens our perspective, sensitizes us to diversity, and fosters empathy.

Gaining Self-Confidence

Ethics Bowl also fosters self-confidence because it does not subscribe to the zero-sum paradigm that underlies many competitive events: "I don't win unless the other side loses." It's very difficult to maintain self-confidence in these high-stakes situations in which only one person (or team) takes all. In Ethics Bowl, in which the goal is to mutually determine the most sound arguments, the task is much less daunting. Students can take on tasks pitched at the level of their own comfort: some can take more supportive, background roles, for example—as we discussed in the section above on public speaking—until they scale up their confidence to gradually assume more responsibility for the success of the team. Microsuccesses are important steps to building self-confidence.

Students' self-confidence is also bolstered because of the unique interaction with adults that Ethics Bowl provides. Take team coaches, most often faculty members. During class time, especially in traditional classes, teachers often disseminate information and students listen. During Ethics Bowl prep, which typically stretches out over three to six months, students are encouraged—expected—to speak their own minds, to offer their opinions about timely, serious, important "adult" issues that often aren't included in the syllabus. Coaches may guide and facilitate, but they don't provide the answers.

Adults who volunteer—moderators and judges as well as observers who attend the matches—also bolster students' self-confidence simply by showing up. For many Ethics Bowlers, participating in a Bowl may provide the first opportunity they have to find themselves in a room full of adults, not necessarily family, who take them seriously. During the judges' questions portion of the match, students may find themselves defending their position or unpacking a complex argument to adults who clearly don't know as much about the issue.

On its own, this type of encounter can build self-confidence as students learn that adults don't have all the answers. Grown-ups can be muddled, biased, and uninformed too. Not everyone thinks clearly. Especially when we talk about ethical dilemmas, no one has all the answers.

At the end of countless matches, judges and observers are often so taken with the high quality of the dialogue that they commend the teams personally. Many of us in the Ethics Bowl community have witnessed a judge or observer approach a team after a match to say, "Wow, that was so impressive! You brought up so many ideas I hadn't considered!" When students feel as if they are taken seriously in this way, their self-confidence grows.

Becoming Resilient

There are two ways in which Ethics Bowl helps students develop resilience, both related to learning how to lose. First, an Ethics Bowl coach can help participants begin to see that we can define "winning" independently of external rewards. Sure, only one team takes home a trophy at the end of an Ethics Bowl season, but those of us in the community know that few students go home feeling like losers.

The paradox coiled at the heart of Ethics Bowl is that most students realize that there are rewards of the event that outweigh the tangible rewards of winning. That's why so many teams that perennially finish in the bottom half or even quarter of the rankings show up year after year. These students have learned to uncover the pleasure of engaging in activity that is hard, that challenges them, in which they are the final judges of what they've learned. Students see themselves speaking up more, feeling confident in their positions, holding their own in heated discussions with peers and adults.

Ethics Bowl also helps students "learn to lose" by affording coaches an opportunity to distinguish between types of losses. In my experience, when both teams are well prepared, the match almost always comes down to a few points and the judges' vote is often split. When matches are this close, it is very easy for students to see that in the end, judging is arbitrary. We've all heard teams leave a match they've lost, trying to rationalize their loss by saying, "The other team had the *easy* case. If we had that case we would have won!" or "If that judge hadn't been so conservative (or so liberal) we would have won."

And in some cases, the students are right! There is an element of dumb luck, or the luck of the draw, in every judged event. One of the two cases discussed during any given Ethics Bowl round may be harder than the other—despite the fact that the organizers take great pains to equalize the level of difficulty. Some judges, even though advised to leave their personal opinions at the door, can't overcome or may not even be aware of their own implicit biases.

When coaches explain this and then help team members acknowledge how much they gained even when losing, students learn about loss more generally. Loss is easier to deal with when you realize that it basically had nothing whatsoever to do with you, who you are as a person, or how you performed. Good students who are prepared and have a good work ethic are still going to experience a great deal of failure in life that comes down to chance or luck. Ethics Bowlers are also prepared to realize that success can't always be measured by external standards.

Courage and Ethical Leadership

Ethics Bowl nurtures all the skills we have discussed above—the ability to become more ethically aware and discerning, to reason and make decisions based on ethical considerations rather than convention or bias, and to engage with others in a collaborative attempt to pose more trenchant questions and suggest more convincing answers. Years of research have shown that people who develop these skills succeed in their careers, are identified as effective leaders, and are more likely to demonstrate ethical courage.

The world has become an increasingly polarized and hostile place. We need people guided by ethical principles who can engage in hard conversations to collaboratively come up with solutions to the problems we all face. We also need people with the courage to stand up for what is right. Ethics Bowl is one of the best activities I can think of to develop these capacities. Preparing a student for life is about preparing them to be courageous, ethical leaders. That's why Ethics Bowl is about so much more than learning how to win arguments. Ethics bowl truly is preparation for life.

***

> My interest in Ethics Bowl began with my desire to grow my own ethical intuition through discussion with my peers. Because ethics deals with intersubjectivity, understanding ethics comes about through connection with others. Ethics Bowl is not like "King of the Hill," where you declare your position on an ethical matter and defend it to the last. Ethics Bowl is the process of engaging in conversation to build moral frameworks, often from the ground up, that address some of the most polarizing issues of our day. Through Ethics Bowl, I learned that often—through deliberation, conversation, and a strong dose of intellectual humility—when faced with

a contemporary moral dilemma, a committed group will be able to find a solution to the most complex issue.

—Josiah Alderink, Intercollegiate Ethics Bowl alumnus

Chapter 9

Room for All

Inclusivity and the High School Ethics Bowl

Jana Mohr Lone

To make "people feel comfortable and welcome the moment they walk in the door." This is how Jana Mohr Lone defines the essence of inclusivity when applied to any event, including Ethics Bowl. Inclusivity is unquantifiable, more elusive to pin down than diversity. Hard to achieve? Yes, but not impossible, as this chapter will explain. To create an event that is truly welcoming, to reward open-mindedness and fluid thinking over polished presentations, takes hours of reflection, and a dedication to experimentation that has always been at the heart of Ethics Bowl and one that needs to remain a core value.

* * *

Since 2014, the University of Washington Center for Philosophy for Children has been organizing and running the Washington State High School Ethics Bowl. From the beginning, the bowl has been relatively large, typically involving twenty or more teams. It's been a successful program from many perspectives. The winner of our bowl generally attends the National High School Ethics Bowl in the spring.

Equity has always been one of our primary concerns. For example, after the first year, we reduced the number of teams each school could send to the Bowl from three to two so that more schools could participate. We worked hard to develop an event that attracts a wide range of participants, extensively recruiting at many public high schools with highly diverse student populations, and giving presentations about the program.

We also let schools know that philosophy graduate students (or advanced undergraduate students) from the University of Washington could serve as Ethics Bowl coaches if no faculty member was available. We sought to broaden our pool of judges by reaching out to relevant campus, nonprofit, and legal organizations. However, the event was still not gaining the level of diversity of participants we had hoped to achieve.

As well, we noted that the performances of the students from private schools often indicated they had spent much more time perfecting their presentations than had many public school students, particularly those situated in low-income areas who were more likely to have, among other things, after-school jobs and sibling childcare responsibilities. Despite our best intentions, an uneven playing field between private and public schools persisted.

Additionally, we observed that many judges tended to award higher scores to students who delivered prepared presentations and made strong arguments for particular resolutions to cases. Because the Ethics Bowl is all about dialogue—it is not debate or an advocacy exercise—we stress to judges that polished presentations advocating for a particular point of view should not be favored over students demonstrating greater flexibility and openness in their thinking and reasoning.

Nevertheless, it was apparent that judges were frequently disposed to reward advocacy-style approaches. Many judges are familiar with debate and mock trial, and in many ways the Ethics Bowl in its outward form resembles these competitions: two teams, judges, presentations, and responses. But at its core, the Ethics Bowl values students' collaborative engagement with one another. Helping students switch gears from the more ubiquitous adversarial model to a dialogic model can be challenging. Helping judges switch gears in the same way can prove even more challenging.

CHANGING THE PARADIGM

After the 2015 Bowl, one high school student who had participated asked if he could help us develop and improve the event as part of his senior project. He created brief surveys for all Ethics Bowl coaches and students that provided us with many suggestions for improvement. After completing the survey, one teacher at a participating public high school—one that is highly diverse and in which approximately 80 percent of the students come from low-income households—sent him an email:

> As the only two teams at the event comprised entirely of students of color, and with all but one of my students speaking a language other than English at home, my students felt out of place and misunderstood among an overwhelmingly

white group of competitors. In addition, the judges were largely older white male attorneys and in their judging they tended to favor mock-trial and debate-team-style presentations, rather than the format outlined in the Ethics Bowl guidelines.

My students came away feeling that they were not judged for their ethical reasoning, but largely on style points, or worse, on their superficial or linguistic difference from the rest of the competitors. The Ethics Bowl has a lot of work to do to be more inclusive and welcoming to a diverse group of students, starting with diversifying their judges and recruiting more heavily among schools with diverse student populations.

Reaching out to this teacher, we proposed that we talk about ways to make the event more appealing to a wider group of participants. This led to a series of discussions among many of the people involved in the Ethics Bowl, including teachers and students.

We realized that we had work to do to make the Ethics Bowl program more inclusive. Inclusivity is not the same thing as diversity. Diversity can be measured; inclusivity is more subtle and less quantifiable. To create an inclusive program does not simply entail inviting people from a broad range of backgrounds to become involved; it requires creating an environment in which people feel comfortable and welcome the moment they walk in the door. A program's venue and practices—the people involved, the way those leading and participating talk and act and think, and what is valued and not valued—are the barometers that determine whether the atmosphere at an event is inclusive or exclusive. Developing an inclusive program involves listening to diverse perspectives, being open to new ideas, and a willingness to change the way things are done.

A DIFFERENT ENVIRONMENT

Analyzing the details of the Bowl, we noted that three of its features detracted from its dialogical goals, preventing it from being the inclusive, inviting event we envisioned: scoring, preparation time and research, and the structure of the rounds. We started with the scoring. Judges and students alike had been confused by the seemingly overly complex system according to which teams could be awarded as many as sixty points. We revamped the scoring rubric, using only thirty-five points as the highest score. This helped judges make their determinations and mitigated problems that had arisen when some judges scored teams much higher or lower than others. We also cut the number of scoring categories and further simplified the instructions.

Next, we considered the fact that students in more affluent schools tended to spend more time preparing for the Bowl than those in less affluent schools. On the one hand, we didn't want to deter preparation time. After all, one of the program's core objectives is creating opportunities for young people to engage in dialogue about ethics and gain skills to think philosophically. Preparation time is valuable—students analyze cases thoroughly from multiple approaches, research precedents and relevant facts, learn about logic and reasoning, and understand how to recognize and construct counterexamples.

On the other hand, disparities in preparation time can cause other equity issues to arise, diminishing the prospects for true dialogue among the students. As one private school teacher put it, "It isn't ideal when private school kids come in dressed up and ready to shout 'Kant' and 'ontology' at other students."

We also observed that students whose presentations weren't as polished as others were nevertheless well able to "think on their feet," responding with insight and creativity. To allow these skills to emerge more readily, we decided in 2017 to introduce a round in which the teams would discuss cases for which neither had prepared. We increased the time that both teams could confer about the cases before the presentations began. The round has helped to level the playing field, offering all the students to showcase their abilities to think in the moment. It has proven hugely popular. In some ways it is the most exciting round, and several schools—both public and private—have requested that more rounds include "cold cases."

In terms of research, we clarified that teams could of course research the cases to provide context and deepen their understanding of the issues; however, during the Bowl, teams could not rely on external facts to support their arguments because neither the judges nor the other team are able to confirm the accuracy of outside facts. Additionally, we asked the presenting team to identify the ethical question(s) most important to the case and address those in their presentation rather than providing the question for them.

Finally, we decided that six teams would participate in semifinal rounds rather than four to allow more teams access to more rounds.

OPEN DIALOGUE

By 2019, we felt as if our Ethics Bowl was significantly more inclusive than when it began, genuinely welcoming a broad range of people, perspectives, and ideas. In 2020, our first, second, and third place teams were all from public schools. The high school teacher who in 2015 had written the email about his students' discomfort with the event commented:

All the changes made by the Center for Philosophy for Children have led to more multiracial teams from a cross section of schools in our region participating and moving on to the final rounds, including the first public school team comprised of a majority of students of color winning the state competition in 2018. My students sometimes still remark on the odd feeling of being among the only black and brown faces in the event, and on how judges' biases against linguistic difference or presentation styles might have played a role in how one round or another turned out.

But they are also winning more rounds year after year and talk proudly and excitedly about how well they did and how close they came to moving on to the next round. And how *next year* will be the one where they make it to the finals. Because they are having fun and they see how they can improve and they want to come back. I don't think this would have been the case if not for the changes the Center for Philosophy for Children continues to put into place.

Although we were proud of our accomplishments, challenges remained. For example, judges still seemed to value polished presentations more than flexible, creative engagement. We needed to help judges embrace dialogue over practiced advocacy.

Part of the problem was inherent in the event's format. Ethics Bowls are highly structured—presentation, commentary, response. As a result, the teams often focus more on performance than conversation; that is, they don't really engage with each other. We were asking judges to evaluate students based on their contribution to a dialogue—on the flexibility of their thinking and their consideration of the other team's point of view—when the structure was not one that encouraged genuine exchanges. In a real dialogue, there is room to think out loud with each other. In fact, the most meaningful give-and-take generally took place during the judges' questions portion of the event when team members engaged with adults and not with one another.

We wanted to give students the opportunity to really talk to each other. In 2019, we instituted another new section in each round that we call "Open Dialogue." After the presentation, commentary, and response and before judges' questions, the teams have five minutes for a self-moderated open dialogue. That first year, we were a bit apprehensive. Would the students talk with one another naturally and openly? Would the moderator be able just to observe and keep time and be otherwise uninvolved? Would the dialogue be thoughtful and substantive?

At first, the Open Dialogue section of the round began tentatively, but the students quickly warmed to the format. By the end of the day, it was clear that offering this dialogical space was a transformative move, addressing two challenges at once. First, the students engaged in genuine discussion the way we hoped they would; their feedback about the new section was uniformly enthusiastic. Second, the judges, hearing the students' thoughtful and open exchanges, came to better understand the collaborative essence of the Ethics Bowl.

Adding Open Dialogue improved another problem area of the Bowl that had bothered us for years: how to score the Civil Dialogue award so that it was truly meaningful. It always troubled us that points in this category were awarded based on a shallow interpretation of civility; that is, for voicing somewhat superficial, performative statements such as, "We thought you made many interesting points," or "Thank you for your presentation." Now, the award points for this category are based on the quality of the teams' engagement in Open Dialogue, which makes civility a far more central and meaningful component of the Bowl.

DURING THE PANDEMIC

In response to the COVID-19 pandemic and the challenges our high school teachers and coaches were facing, the Washington State Ethics Bowl changed significantly in 2020. After consulting with all our coaches, we decided not to hold a formal event in 2021 but instead arranged a series of two-hour virtual scrimmages between schools to take place between April and June 2021. Some schools began to prepare in the fall; others waited until winter.

Two cases were discussed during each scrimmage. The format included a presentation, a commentary on the presentation, and a ten-minute open dialogue (rather than five minutes as in previous years), followed by judges' questions. (We omitted the response to commentary.) In perhaps the most substantial change, scrimmages were not scored. Instead, the judges provided detailed feedback at the end of each session during which students were encouraged to ask the judges questions, often leading to extended conversations.

We plan to retain many of these innovations. The longer Open Dialogue interval seems to induce richer, more engaging discussions. We will also omit the response to commentary as a stand-alone portion of a round because we discovered that students naturally comment on each other's presentations and commentaries during Open Dialogue and that these exchanges tended to be far more substantive.

We never expected that a virtual Ethics Bowl would prove more personal than in-person Bowls, but in some ways this turned out to be the case. During virtual scrimmages, all the students were in their own Zoom windows with their names and school names displayed. As a result, students from different teams were able to speak directly to one another, frequently referring to each other by name. Although students had worn name tags in the past, we hadn't noticed such direct engagement. Moving forward, we are considering giving students table tents displaying their names that they would carry from room to room to enable this more direct, personal conversation. We are also thinking about ways to incorporate verbal feedback at the end of each round since it was such a positive aspect of the scrimmages for both judges and students.

FUTURE DIRECTIONS

Holding the Ethics Bowl during the pandemic was gratifying in ways we never expected, revealing to us just how close a community had been created over the course of seven years. Although some schools were initially interested in participating in a more traditional Ethics Bowl event (albeit online) and were equipped to do so, coaches and students demonstrated their commitment to hold the event in whatever form was best for everyone—in keeping with the camaraderie and cooperative nature of the program. In September, when we began the email conversation about what to do for the year, one private school coach wrote:

> I have a budget for the Ethics Club, the school loves us, and I realize we have more resources than other local schools. I attended public schools and taught in them, so I personally have a desire to help others with any resources we may be able to provide. This is an Ethics Club after all. I am unsure what that looks like, but maybe in the future if restrictions have loosened up, we could provide a space for something. I have a whole lot of student leaders that could help organize optional sessions with other schools.

Clearly, the Washington State High School Ethics Bowl had become a program in which the schools involved thought of themselves less as competitors than as part of a collective effort to bring ethical dialogue into the lives of as many young people as possible.

During the pandemic, the program was not a competition: no scoring and no winners. Many of the adults—and students—who participated commented on the depth of the dialogue and the more relaxed, open atmosphere. Yet when I ask coaches and students about removing competition from the Ethics Bowl in the future, it is clear that this would not be a popular change. Instead, we will continue to explore new ways to build an inclusive competitive program that fosters dialogue and collaborative thinking, introducing further innovations that honor diverse perspectives and student voices.

* * *

Growing up, I was introverted, refusing to speak up for myself in fear of judgment from others. I didn't think my voice mattered. However, after my friends encouraged me to join our school's Ethics Bowl team during my sophomore year, my perspective changed drastically. Participating in Ethics Bowl with my peers and under the guidance of supportive teachers has molded me into the person that I am today. I became close friends and developed strong connections with all of my teammates, who became a second family to me. Through Ethics Bowl I have learned valuable communication skills and to respect different people's perspectives. But most importantly, Ethics Bowl has taught me that my voice matters to others, that I can make important and insightful contributions. Through Ethics Bowl I was able to cultivate my passion for debate and politics, inspiring me to pursue a field in law. Ethics Bowl has provided me with the skills, both in my future career and in developing relationships with others, in order to become successful.

—Sara Manandhar, High School Ethics Bowler

PART III

Expanding the Reach of Ethics Bowl

Chapter 10

The "Turn to Reason"
Ethics Bowl in the Classroom

William M. Beals, Christina Drogalis, and Morgan E. Wallhagen

Ever since its inception, Ethics Bowl has proven its adaptability. As we've seen, there are many ways to make it a more accessible and equitable event. Additionally, its core methodology—asking participants to "turn to reason" when confronted with a dilemma, and to thoughtfully consider other points of view—can be adapted for classroom use. When it is employed as a deliberative pedagogy, as the authors of this chapter explain, preparing for Ethics Bowl supplements classroom activities, which in turn helps students prepare for Ethics Bowl, creating a virtuous circle.

* * *

Ethics Bowl has played an important role at our school, Stanford Online High School, since we began a club six years ago. Our school is unusual in a few ways: we are an online institution with an international student body and require that full-time students take a sequence of yearlong philosophy courses called Core Classes.

This last feature has played a significant role in our positive experience with Ethics Bowl in two ways. First, because most of our students have been taking philosophy courses for several years, they are naturally drawn to joining the club and already have many necessary skills for Ethics Bowl. Second, participation in Ethics Bowl has helped our students develop skills that we consider important in our general curriculum. We've found that students who enjoy and do well in Ethics Bowl tend to also do well in our philosophy courses, and vice versa.

Our Core curriculum includes ninth and tenth grade classes that focus primarily on thinking about biology and science from a philosophical perspective. We intend to introduce our students to philosophical thinking in an interdisciplinary way through other subject areas that may be more familiar to them. Next, students take an eleventh grade political philosophy course and, in twelfth grade, a class akin to a college Introduction to Philosophy class. In these courses, we introduce students to more traditional texts from the history of philosophy and contemporary philosophy, and build upon the reading, writing, and discussion skills that they've begun to develop in earlier courses.

One of the most significant commonalities between our courses and Ethics Bowl is the way in which students encounter views that are different from their own, put forward by intelligent peers. In many settings, disagreement is common enough, but in the context of Ethics Bowl and our classes, students are encouraged (indeed required!) to offer reasons for their positions. These reasons are intended to be compelling to anyone prepared to listen, not only people with philosophical knowledge and training.

When students disagree, then, they don't simply reiterate their initial view—their immediate gut reaction, or initial impulse about what is right or wrong or true or false. Instead, they appeal to reasons to resolve the disagreement, to try as best as they can to present more convincing evidence and persuasive considerations to support their positions. They are called upon to think about why one should, rationally speaking, accept one position rather than the other.

THE TURN TO REASON

This "turn to reason" is an important moment in the development of any sophisticated thinker. But in the context of resolving disagreement, the pressure to appeal to reason also promotes a deeper understanding of both one's own views and those of others. This may lead a student to reconsider her position—because the reasons she puts forth in support of her view might not, after all, seem so plausible.

Or, even if her initial reasons seem plausible, tracing back her reasons yet further, she may become aware of her "basic premises"—those notions, ideas or beliefs that are fundamental to her own ethical thinking. Perhaps she realizes that even if these are intuitively plausible, another outcome is possible, or even likely. She may discover that they are not self-evident and that other starting points are at the very least reasonable (to the extent that they are not internally inconsistent or otherwise incoherent).

Much the same can result from hearing out her interlocutor. As she puts forward reasons for her position, she may come to appreciate how another view does indeed follow from more basic beliefs that are not ridiculous or absurd and may even resonate with her in various ways.

In this chapter, we will expand upon the ways that Ethics Bowl has helped to supplement our Core curriculum and its goals. We will also focus on the ways in which what we teach in our Core classes has led to our students developing skills necessary for success in Ethics Bowl. As we'll discuss, students benefit from participating in Ethics Bowl whether or not their teams do well competitively.

However, we believe that when Ethics Bowl rounds proceed as intended, successful teams exemplify the intellectual virtues that all disciplines (to some degree) value. In this way, the competitive aspect of Ethics Bowl can encourage students to develop important skills and traits regardless of whether they "win" any particular round. In what follows, then, we hope to give other high school educators ideas about how Ethics Bowl can help to support their pedagogical goals and lead them to consider adding philosophy classes to more curricula, even in schools that are quite different from ours.

HOW WHAT WE TEACH IN CLASS SUPPORTS ETHICS BOWL

Our school's uniqueness is rooted not only in the fact that it is taught fully online, but also in its commitment to make philosophy a required part of the curriculum. Through our experience teaching philosophy courses and coaching Ethics Bowl teams, we are confident that there is a deep, thoroughgoing connection between the critical thinking skills taught in our philosophy courses and the skills honed in Ethics Bowl such that development in one area supports development in the other.

Although we realize that it is unlikely that philosophy courses will become a required part of school curricula broadly any time soon, the critical thinking skills central to philosophy and Ethics Bowl can be cultivated in diverse ways. This makes our reflections on our experience relevant beyond our own specific pedagogical choices and methods. At a high level of abstraction, all instruction does (or at least can) involve two basic features that are relevant to Ethics Bowl and rigorous thought generally: thoughtful discussion and the clear presentation of reasoning and evidence in support of a conclusion. Those who teach philosophy, English, chemistry, or calculus all have the opportunity to engage and interact with students in ways that will allow them to develop their abilities to communicate their thoughts in inquisitive, probing, thoughtful, and rigorous ways.

We will now focus on how teaching philosophy through discussion-based classes with thesis-driven, argumentative papers contributes to critical thinking skills relevant to Ethics Bowl and beyond.

Perhaps the greatest similarity between our classes and Ethics Bowl is that discussion is central to both. Our class format requires students to prepare for class by reading—and occasionally watching prerecorded lectures on—the material. During class discussions, we typically ask students to reconstruct the main arguments and ideas from the material and then to subject those arguments and ideas to critical scrutiny. Students are encouraged to not only respond to the instructor's guiding questions, but also to respond to the thoughts of their fellow students by adding support to ideas they find promising and objecting to those they find unconvincing. All are conducted in a collegial, cooperative spirit.

For example, in the beginning of the second semester of our eleventh grade political philosophy course, we read John Stuart Mill's classic *On Liberty*. We cover a chapter of the book for each class meeting, and students are asked to give an account of the argument presented and subject the argument to critique. As students become familiar with this style of critical engagement with a text, it is often unnecessary to prompt them with critical questions.

Upon reading Mill's argument in favor of limiting individuals' liberty only when doing so is necessary to prevent harm, students will, often without prompting, begin to probe Mill's notion of harm: Is it too narrow? How does it account for hate speech? How might it be enriched in such a way as to be more satisfying? Is such enrichment consistent with Mill's foundational standard of utility? How might Mill (or a defender of Mill's theory) respond to these objections and suggestions?

Invariably, students stake out divergent views in response. This divergence prompts a deeper discussion. Students are expected to defend their views, but also listen to the claims of others. When a student changes her or his view—and to our great satisfaction, this does happen—it usually results from listening to and reflecting on the ideas of others.

Anyone familiar with the principles of Ethics Bowl and their realization in a particular match will see the connection between them and this brief description of the structure of our class discussions.

Our teams have been consistently strong in these rounds. Team members listen attentively to the ideas of others and respond thoughtfully. Whether or not the team resists a change in its analysisafter the exchange, the response is rarely dogmatic. Instead, team members demonstrate that they have heard what others have said and responded in light of what they think is most rationally convincing with the aid of the others' comments.

A recent round at the Northern California Regional Ethics Bowl strikingly illustrated the tight connection between our practices in class and those in

Ethics Bowl. In this match, two of our teams met in the semifinal round. This was an exciting, if not also fraught, experience. One of the more remarkable features of it, though, was how *similar* it was to our class meetings in so many ways relevant to the practice of critical thinking.

Despite its centrality, class discussion is not the only mode of cultivating student development relevant to Ethics Bowl skills in class. Written assignments, especially major argumentative papers, promote students' abilities to clearly state a position, support it, and defend it against objections.

For example, one such assignment prompted students to apply John Stuart Mill's philosophical defense of political liberty—in particular, freedom of speech—to a current event such as "cancel culture" and critically evaluate what it would dictate. Whether students defend or reject the legitimacy of Mill's framework, they are expected to do so citing reasons and evidence and with sensitivity to alternative points of view.

Written assignments such as this, along with the structure of class discussions, cultivate students' abilities to construct and defend arguments, skills relevant to success in Ethics Bowl and beyond. Considering and responding to possible objections certainly prepares them for thinking imaginatively and creatively about how those who might disagree with them would evaluate the relevant issue. As well, the practice of paper writing is perhaps even more relevant for the first portion of an Ethics Bowl presentation during which participants give their reasoned position on a case.

More specifically, the structure common to our students' papers serves them very well in Ethics Bowl, during which they clearly present the essentials of the case, the reasoning behind their answer to the question raised about it, and consider and respond to likely objections. To our delight, several Ethics Bowl judges have told us that they admired the clarity of our teams' presentations, saying that it enriched and deepened the ensuing discussion.

Of course, not every class in every discipline is going to be as directly relevant to Ethics Bowl—in terms of content—as a course involving political theory. However, all subjects require that students communicate and reason well in order to do well. John Stuart Mill does not have to be on the syllabus to reinforce this.

HOW WHAT WE PRACTICE IN ETHICS BOWL IMPACTS STUDENTS IN CLASS

Not only do the distinctive aspects of our classroom, school, and curriculum inform students' experience in Ethics Bowl, as discussed above; participating in Ethics Bowl helps students' classroom performance regardless of the format (physical vs. online) or topic (philosophy, history, English, etc.).

As teachers and coaches, we are convinced Ethics Bowl team members develop the intellectual qualities that are important in any classroom, and prepare them for the work they are expected to do in any critical discipline. In particular, we believe that participation in the Bowl especially helps students develop the capacity to (1) give and assess reasons, (2) engage in constructive discussion of contentious issues, and (3) listen attentively to one's interlocutor to genuinely engage with the ideas under discussion. We'll comment on each of these points in turn.

Giving and assessing reasons, along with the interconnected habits of considering other perspectives and reflecting carefully on one's own commitments, are not, of course, unique to Ethics Bowl. Indeed, these are the very intellectual skills that we hope to inculcate in our students in many of our high school classes. Still, what makes Ethics Bowl distinctive is the way it promotes sustained, repeated, and respectful efforts to engage in these sorts of acts. Successfully developing any skill, including intellectual skills, depends on practice and on receiving timely feedback. Ethics Bowl provides both. It requires teams to meet frequently and engage in practice rounds to prepare their cases, and to incorporate coaches' feedback.

The competitive element of Ethics Bowl is beneficial. Students are likely to be "rewarded" (with a win) for particularly strong displays of good reasoning, clear expression, careful listening, and thoughtful assessment. They are likely to be "punished" (with a loss) for less impressive displays of one or more of those habits.

Keep in mind that teams are not assessed for the particular ethical position they defend. For one thing, "opposing" teams may advance the same position on a given case. More telling, it is possible to win a round even when the judges disagree with the winning team's determination about the ethically correct action that should be taken in a given case. Judges are instructed to evaluate teams not on the basis of which position they defend, but on the clarity, precision, and forcefulness of their exposition and the reasonableness of their response to questions from the other team and the judges. As well, teams may be rewarded for modifying their position in response to a reasonable objection, or docked for dogmatically refusing to adjust their stance.

Jon Ellis, Associate Professor of Philosophy and Director of the Center for Public Philosophy at UC Santa Cruz, reinforced this point in his opening remarks at the annual Northern California Regional Ethics Bowl Competition. He explained that Ethics Bowl differs from traditional debate competitions in two important ways: by discouraging *motivated reasoning*—reasoning intentionally designed to support a position one already accepts—and by encouraging open-minded discussion aimed to discover the most reasonable position.

In sum, Ethics Bowls encourage students to exhibit the very sorts of intellectual habits of mind we would like to see them exhibit in writing, speech, and thinking. We believe that Ethics Bowl is particularly effective at inculcating and enhancing these good habits of careful, critical thought, at least in part, *because* it is competitive. Students who participate in Ethics Bowl, quite naturally, want to do well, and doing well depends on their ability to deploy the core intellectual skills we have been discussing. The prospect of doing well motivates them to exhibit those qualities and offers the sort of timely feedback necessary to promote the development of those skills. We hope these points may sway some who otherwise find the idea of competitive debate and discussion about ethical questions (at least somewhat) distasteful.

Participating in Ethics Bowl also helps students develop their discussion skills. As every teacher knows, some students who shine in written work "clam up" in class; writing skills don't always translate into good discussion skills. In-class discussion can help, but Ethics Bowl is particularly effective in this area since verbal discussion is its primary medium of thought. Students talk with each other as they work to understand the cases and develop their positions, when they present their cases during the event—which includes raising questions for the other team—and when they reply to questions from the other team and the judges.

Especially during the actual events, clear and concise expression is crucial. In developing their case, students with different perspectives present their views and adjust their position or compromise so that the team can come up with a coherent presentation—even if they recognize that objections or outstanding issues remain.

Productive discussion in Ethics Bowl, in turn, helps students develop their listening skills. Team members must listen carefully to one another as they develop their case and work out disagreements. And again, careful listening is particularly important during the event itself. Performance in these rounds is based partly on how well teams respond to questions from the other team and from judges. Failure to answer the question asked, or failure to recognize a compelling point and adjust one's position appropriately, can be the difference between winning or losing. Ethics Bowl thus promotes careful listening and close attention to the meaning and relevance of what one's interlocutor is saying.

Careful attention, clear expression, the give-and-take of reasons, compromising, adjusting, or standing firm where appropriate: these are the elements of positive, productive discourse, all enhanced through the Ethics Bowl experience. All of this, we believe, feeds back into the classroom. Though chains of cause and effect can be difficult to disentangle, we have at least anecdotal evidence of students becoming more confident, poised contributors to class discussions as a result of participating in Ethics Bowl.

For example, one of us had two students from the same Ethics Bowl team in two of his classes during the 2020–2021 academic year. Over the course of that year, he witnessed clear improvement in their ability to communicate with each other and to listen and respond to feedback constructively. Although these two particular students had a tendency to clash heads, both ideologically and stylistically, their ability to work collaboratively improved. Very likely, their participation on an Ethics Bowl team contributed to this.

Ethics Bowl participants, by and large, more clearly understand ethical theories, and more deeply appreciate ethically relevant considerations, both in their speech and writing, than their classmates who do not participate. They also tend to consider, with more open minds, alternative ideas during class discussions and argue more rigorously in their writing. Anecdotal evidence? Yes—but it seems compelling nonetheless because these are the skills we would expect to be enhanced by participation in Ethics Bowl for the reasons noted above. We fully expect, moreover, that these skills will be enhanced whether students are learning in a physical or online classroom, and have an impact on students' abilities and performance across a wide range of disciplines.

* * *

Participating in Ethics Bowl has improved both my perspective on the world as well as my perspective of teammates. The ability to represent my school in the National High School Ethics Bowl was an honor and a very formative experience that has changed me for the better not only in my thinking but also in my ability to work with others. In my thinking I have learned to contemplate the ideas of others and how to counter those ideas with which I disagree, and this has helped me in my writing as well as my overall perspective. In my teamwork since the Bowl, I have noticed that I work better with my teammates and have established bonds with new people as a result.

—Shane Bennett, High School Ethics Bowler

Chapter 11

Deliberating across the Lifespan

Michael Vazquez

Ethics Bowls always involved adults—as coaches and judges. But why not compose adult Ethics Bowl teams? Many people who judge or coach leave an event wondering when they will have the opportunity to answer questions instead of ask them. According to Parr Center for Ethics Director of Outreach Michael Vazquez, Ethics Bowls can be adapted in a variety of settings (workplace, senior centers) and across a wide swath of professions.

* * *

As a person advances in age, doesn't he become increasingly reluctant to sing? That is, he enjoys it less and, when compelled to do it, he feels especially embarrassed—the more so the older and more moderate he has become. Isn't this so?[1]

FLIP THE SCRIPT: ETHICS BOWL FOR ADULTS

The young are malleable. Educable. Their prospects for growth and achievement are vast and filled with promise. Adults, on the other hand, are hardened—worn down by experience, too busy for leisure and play, too fixed in their ways to learn new things.

So goes a familiar story about aging, at least. It is well past time for outreach practitioners to flip the script. The same optimism that motivated the pioneers of the Philosophy for Children movement to dismantle educational prejudices toward children should animate our efforts to work with folks beyond the schooling years. We must continue to think expansively about who has a seat at the table in the "community of philosophical inquiry"[2]—and Ethics Bowl is one of the best tools for the job.

Ethics Bowl is an opportunity for individuals to engage in ethical reflection *for themselves* and to, thereby, have greater ownership over their habits, beliefs, values, and life projects. It is also an opportunity for individuals to cultivate democratic skills and dispositions that will in turn permeate the civic sphere, the workplace, and other domains of shared life. In this way, Ethics Bowl for Adults is both a space for humanistic self-fulfillment and for the ameliorative project of maintaining and transforming the social order by producing more ethical professionals and more public-spirited citizens.

Unlike general philosophy discussion activities, Ethics Bowl is an exercise in *deliberation*.[3] Deliberation centers on the question, "What should I *do*?" construed broadly so as to include interpersonal ethical choices that arise in the context of everyday life, controversial policy questions, and other individual and collective decision points that involve trade-offs, competing values, preferences, risks, obligations, and other features of practical import. Ethics Bowl provides a space for folks to *practice* deliberating by "giving reasons, listening, considering perspectives, evaluating views, and treating each other as political equals."[4] This is why we should not hesitate to call Ethics Bowl a *deliberative pedagogy*.[5]

Engrained assumptions about age, plasticity, and decline have so far prevented us from exploiting the power of this pedagogical tool for the promotion of lifelong learning, a cause championed by the educational theorist Eduard Lindeman in the twentieth century:

> From many quarters comes the call to a new kind of education with its initial assumption affirming that *education is life*—not a mere preparation for an unknown kind of future living . . . The whole of life is learning, therefore education can have no endings. This new venture is called *adult education*—not because it is confined to adults but because adulthood, maturity, defines its limits.[6]

Lindeman gives pride of place to "the learner's experience" as opposed to passive forms of content acquisition.[7] His focus on inquiry that is guided by real-world needs, interests, and puzzles is well-suited to Ethics Bowl as a discursive form of case-based reasoning.

Ethics Bowl is, in essence, a structured and curated environment for discussion of the sort Lindeman envisioned: a "co-operative venture in non-authoritarian, informal learning," and a vehicle for egalitarian associations among adults centered on the cultivation of democratic habits of thought, talk, and action.[8] The fate of our democratic experiment depends not only on our commitment to the education of the next generation, but also on our commitment to creating opportunities for the present generation to adapt and to grow in the face of ever-changing circumstances.[9]

STRATEGIES FOR PROSPECTIVE ORGANIZERS

As a deliberative pedagogy, Ethics Bowl is more than any particular set of rules and procedures. Foremost, it is an exercise in humility. The activity begins from a collective recognition of the "hazards involved in the correct (and conscientious) exercise of our powers of reason and judgment"[10] and an acknowledgment that reasonable and well-intentioned people can disagree about questions of value and ethics. It is most fruitfully used to discuss issues around which there is *reasonable disagreement*, or disagreement about matters of ethics and value that persists even after all parties have competently and earnestly reckoned with the same facts and considerations.

Some organizers of Ethics Bowls for adults worry that the regimentation of the activity—scoring, judging, and time constraints—might seem childish. However, whether or not a regimented activity like Ethics Bowl will be perceived as heavy-handed depends on the particular individuals with whom you are engaging. In my ongoing efforts to host Senior Ethics Bowls in North Carolina, some groups of older adults have expressed a preference for retaining traditional elements like scoring and judging. For some, rules and scoring provide structure and additional incentive to participate actively. For others, that is not the case, so it is worth approaching Ethics Bowl for adults with a particular kind of flexibility.

Remember: the aims of Ethics Bowl can be realized in *many* different ways. Extended opportunities to speak, respond, collaborate, and change one's mind are ineliminable features of Ethics Bowl—but there is a great deal of latitude within those constraints. As an organizer you can treat the elements of an Ethics Bowl match ("initial presentation," "commentary," and so on) as modular pieces that can be moved around or used in isolation. It also helps to think of the essential *skills* involved in, for example, analyzing an Ethics Bowl case—offering a responsive commentary or formulating judge questions—as skills that can be promoted in isolation with activities suited to the diverse needs, interests, and constraints of participants.

Finally, it helps to think of Ethics Bowl for adults as an educational *package* that includes didactic elements, normative case studies, and opportunities for discussion. Although adults are uniquely well-situated to discuss ethical dilemmas on the basis of lived experience, an appropriate dose of ethical theory enables participants to impose structure on what is an otherwise diffuse set of moral intuitions and experiences.

A basic repertoire of ethical concepts also provides a shared foundation and vocabulary with which folks can disagree and discuss a case. In all cases it is important to avoid jargon and other needless barriers to entry. Organizers should emphasize the robust expertise participants *already* have, both in virtue of their practical and professional experience, and in virtue of the fact that they are socialized human beings.[11] It is also important to avoid giving the impression that case-based reasoning is nothing more than the mindless application of systematic ethical theories like consequentialism and deontology. Aside from certain forms of consequentialism, it was rarely the intention of moral philosophers to provide a simple decision procedure or algorithm for figuring out what the right thing to do is!

An ethical toolkit for participants should facilitate, rather than inhibit, careful scrutiny of the richness of concrete situations, and it should also be tailored specifically to the discussion at hand. So, for example, an Ethics Bowl for city policymakers centered on the implementation of a proposed randomized control trial for universal basic income might benefit from a crash course on competing principles of distributive justice (e.g., equality, sufficiency, utility, merit) and ethical notions like "paternalism" and "respect."

What Ethics Bowl provides is a domain-general space within which folks can discuss the distinctive ethical issues that arise in the context of their professional practice and everyday lives, with all the nuance and specificity such discussions deserve. As the burgeoning of applied domains of ethical theory in philosophy has demonstrated, every arena of professional practice—whether that is business, policy, medicine, education, or other domains—is pervaded by ethical values and dilemmas.

ETHICS BOWL FOR EDUCATIONAL PROFESSIONALS

Education is a fruitful place to begin since the philosophical and democratic foundations of schooling are in many ways aligned with the core ideals of Ethics Bowl—an activity which began in the classroom, after all! Promising research has demonstrated the theoretical congruence and salutary effects of ethical literacy and deliberative practices like Ethics Bowl for educational practice.[12] There is also innovative work being done at, for example, the Harvard Graduate School of Education to provide teachers and educational leaders with opportunities to reflect on ethical and normative dimensions of their practice. I commend in particular the resources and publications curated by Harvard Graduate School of Education's Justice in Schools Project (www.justiceinschools.org) and the case studies found in Levinson and Fay (2016, 2019). Ethics Bowl provides a ready-made space within which such discussions can take place, with educators and experienced practitioners alike aspiring to enter the profession.

In the summer of 2020, I organized an Ethics Bowl for educational professionals as the capstone event for a doctoral seminar on the Social Foundations of Education. After weeks of reflecting on foundational questions around educational practice—including the aims of education, diversity and multiculturalism, and distributive justice—twenty-five educational professionals were divided into four teams. Each team had the chance to analyze and discuss two cases from Levinson and Fay (2019) and was guided on how to identify the salient normative dimensions of the case, articulate why it might be the basis of reasonable disagreement, and stake out a nuanced position on the issue.[13] The first case focused on the difficulties of facilitating controversial conversations in the classroom, and the second focused on de facto segregation at a charter school founded to meet the needs of a Somali immigrant community. The Ethics Bowl was also followed by an individual writing assignment in which students crafted a normative case study of their own and wrote an "ethics memo" analyzing the case. Two students who were unable to attend the capstone Ethics Bowl were able to conduct a written and asynchronous analogue to Ethics Bowl, complete with presentation, commentary, and judge periods—further testimony to the malleable nature of the Ethics Bowl format.

At the end of the course, students reflected on the value of Ethics Bowl for their professional growth:

1. "As an attorney and a former competitive debater, I learned that participating in this exercise was somewhat difficult because of the less competitive nature that it presented (e.g., I really wanted to cross-examine members of the other team). It's difficult, but I would like to do something like this again with the cohort so we can reach reasoned outcomes and I can work on ridding any vestiges of competitive behavior."
2. "During the process of the 'Ethics Bowl,' I recognized that I'm still stretching to master the skill of assertion without aggression. Monitoring my internal reactions to ideas from my groupmates, I noticed that I was hyperaware about measuring my responses; I wanted to find the 'right' words and tone without compromising what I meant. I like that I'm trying; I think that everybody should do so."
3. "I really learned the power of productive silence in a conversation. Just taking the time to really step back and listen to the other point of view in relation to my own . . ."
4. "I personally loved this format and the way in which it allowed for 'safe' discourse . . . and I don't think [debate] lends itself to the purpose

of having healthy dialogue around complex, triggering, and sensitive issues."

Ethics Bowl for educators has promising curricular and extracurricular use cases. Deliberative democratic practices can be incorporated into standard coursework and training for educators and educational leaders in Schools of Education, or else incorporated into continuing education programming for active professionals and school districts across the country.

One of the most heartening aspects of Ethics Bowl is its propensity to spread. That is, those who experience its transformative value, especially firsthand, tend to advocate for it, whether high school students who talk about it with friends at other schools who then go on to create teams, or midcareer educational professionals who participate in an Ethics Bowl as part of their graduate studies and go on to organize an Ethics Bowl for teachers within their school, or for principals within their school district, or as a school-wide activity intended to build community and foster public deliberation. Judges, as well, recruited as prominent community members, often become Ethics Bowl's biggest proponents, amplifying the program's spread and giving voice to its central tenets. In a word, Ethics Bowl is contagious.

ETHICS BOWL IN THE WORKPLACE

Another promising frontier is to introduce Ethics Bowl into professional development and training opportunities in the workplace. Calls for the cultivation of business ethics are not new, but Ethics Bowl provides a uniquely engaging format and structure for such programming. The process of case preparation and discussion can be compressed into an intensive event or series of meetings that is both didactic and interactive.

The Parr Center continues to offer three-hour credit-bearing workshops for UNC frontline employees in partnership with UNC's Human Resources department. The workshops allowed participants to think through issues and challenges that commonly arise in workplace ethics, including the moral responsibilities of supervisors and supervisees, conflicts of interest, and personal relationships on the job.

The structure of the Ethics Bowl invites a level of nuance and complexity that is all too often lacking in discussion of ethical dilemmas in the workplace. Those who participate can move beyond a professional ethic of rule-compliance and instead discuss the intellectual and moral virtues that can sustain a collaborative, ethical, and respectful workplace *culture*. At the Parr Center, we also hope to leverage our network of private and nonprofit sector partners to offer Ethics Bowl programming in the workplace (e.g., at annual corporate retreats or leadership training workshops).

ETHICS BOWL FOR PUBLIC SERVANTS

In recent years, more of those engaged in the public sector have come to appreciate that philosophy can guide them as they engage with the normative and ethical dimensions of public sector work. One model for Ethics Bowl for public servants, and one that speaks to the possibilities and interest of this kind of programming, took place in the city of Durham, North Carolina. "Ethical Leadership and Decision-Making at All Levels" workshops were offered in response to polling of city employees that expressed concerns about the ethical culture in the city's workforce and low levels of trust in city leadership. The director of Durham's Department of Audit Services, Germaine Brewington, partnered with the Philosophy department at UNC-Chapel Hill to provide case-based and discussion-oriented programming rooted in the elements of Ethics Bowl. Building on the success of this model of programming, Germaine is spearheading our efforts to integrate Ethics Bowl programming into existing educational opportunities for city employees during the workday. As she notes:

> The City's ethics training programs . . . bring awareness to employees about the ethical behavior expected at the City; and they provide City employees a framework to think through ethical dilemmas. Ethics in the workplace also underpins the relationships between the community and City staff because operating under a set of ethics policies helps City employees accurately and equitably manage tax dollars entrusted to them by City residents.

Ethics Bowl for public servants promises to lead to more reflection on ethical issues arising in a distinctive and underappreciated sphere of professional practice. It is also an opportunity to integrate ethics programming with other city-based academic partnerships that aim to keep public servants appraised of cutting-edge social scientific research, create opportunities for normative reflection that is grounded in the complexity of real-world problems, and avoid some of the vices of overly stylized or idealized ethical reasoning in philosophy.

ETHICS BOWL FOR OLDER ADULTS

Ethics Bowl for Older Adults can be fruitfully situated in the context of wider adult programming discussed at the beginning of this chapter, which includes both general philosophical inquiry and the specific kind of practical deliberation that is characteristic of Ethics Bowl.

Ethics Bowl through Informal Discussion

Lindeman was a proponent of small group discussions, and in particular neighborhood discussion groups that he deemed "the finest medium available for dealing with controversial issues."[14] Ethics Bowl can provide infrastructure for democratic community groups of this kind. Take, for example, Bartlett Reserve Retirement Community's "Brainstorming" discussion group in Durham, North Carolina. Formerly known as Socrates Café, we collectively decided to shift our focus to ethical and normative reflection, using case studies from the National High School Ethics Bowl case archive as the anchor for each session. Each of our sessions begin with a guiding question that is the functional equivalent of a moderator question.

Although there are no teams or rounds, many of the didactic and discursive elements of Ethics Bowl are still present. Each case presents an opportunity to introduce canonical ethical notions that are germane to the topic at hand. Each team member has the chance to serve as presenter, respondent, judge, and moderator. We have found that the informal format is especially conducive to earnest, nonperformative discussion. Here's what I mean: during a formal Ethics Bowl match, folks are more inclined to take a broader view on the issue, to consider the issue from different angles and points of view, and to reason in less self-regarding ways. That's a feature, not a bug, of the design of Ethics Bowl as an activity. Sometimes, though, it helps to give those same people the chance to be more forthright than they might in the context of a public dialogue, where candor is mediated by social expectation. The notion that *sincerity* is vital to our collaborative pursuit of truth goes back to Socrates's public philosophizing in Athens.[15] That's where the informal discussion group centered on Ethics Bowl can help.

Senior Ethics Bowls

We are working with retirement communities and older adult advocacy groups in the Triangle area to offer conventional Ethics Bowl programming to seniors. To lower the barrier to entry, it helps to limit scheduled matches to *two* cases chosen democratically by those involved—or slightly more if teams want to preserve the element of surprise on match day. A tip for organizers: the case selection process is fun and rewarding for everyone, and an early opportunity for "opposing teams" to meet. It is also a useful teaching opportunity, for example, to introduce the basic elements of case-based reasoning and ethical analysis.

In our experience, senior enrichment coordinators welcome the opportunity to partner with a local university to offer programming that is accessible, engaging, and, most importantly, well-defined. It is also important to reach older adults who do not live in congregate communities, so we work closely with the Orange County Department of Aging and plan to continue to utilize public senior centers to create deliberative opportunities for folks from different communities and backgrounds.

Keep in mind: Ethics Bowl can be the occasion for forming new community partnerships with communities of older adults, but it can also be introduced to longstanding community partners—for example, as a way to shake up the traditional senior philosophy discussion group or as a capstone event for a group like Bartlett Reserve that is already reading and discussing ethics.

INTERGENERATIONAL ETHICS BOWL

Finally, this past academic year, I designed and taught a new, experiential education course in philosophy that promotes learning across generations and across the lifespan. The course was conceived as a response to the many calls by advocates for older adults to create opportunities for intergenerational encounters that promote well-being, social inclusion, and civic participation. UNC undergraduates participated in weekly hour-long discussions with older adults from the Retired Faculty Association at UNC and from the Galloway Ridge retirement community. Students worked with "intergenerational peer reviewers" to compose public-facing philosophical op-ed pieces. They also planned an intergenerational philosophy capstone event at which groups of undergraduates and older adults deliberated about a case study on forgiveness.

The aim was to grapple with a question that is of particular interest to an intergenerational audience and that implicates central dimensions of our practical and moral lives. Building off the success of this program, our plan is to continue to offer intergenerational experiential education opportunities to UNC undergraduates and to expand intergenerational Ethics Bowl programming to primary and secondary school students. There are exciting prospects for bringing older adults into the fold of existing communities of practice, such as the Middle School Ethics Bowl, the National High School Ethics Bowl, and the Intercollegiate Ethics Bowl. Intergenerational Ethics Bowl admits of several promising variations: older adults deliberating alongside younger students, neighbors and family members deliberating across generations about issues of local concern, and young students using Ethics Bowl as a Civic Action Project for facilitating important conversations in their communities.

We have high hopes for the success of the programs already underway, and we are excited to collaboratively pursue the aspirations outlined in this chapter and elsewhere in the volume. Ethics Bowl remains one of the most impactful forms of public philosophy in our engagement toolkit. It fosters mutual respect and a spirit of cooperation in the face of ethical and political disagreement, and bridges our many divisions—age included.

[See references for this chapter in the References and Resources section.]

* * *

For me, Ethics Bowl was a great learning experience, and one that I would absolutely love to continue participating in. Discussing the overall positions our group would defend for each case developed my abilities to persuade and compromise, while being in the event itself strengthened my ability to debate. I discussed contentious, modern issues in a constructive manner and became more aware of their nuances and similarities to historical issues. I would thoroughly recommend it to anyone interested in public speaking, debate, research, or collaborative work. A word of advice to the newcomer: do not fret about what you don't know when you first receive the cases. As someone who initially panicked about my inexperience and lack of knowledge about factory farming, I am most proud of our performance in the round in which this case was discussed. I was proud to speak to it and provide specific, topical examples of environmentally friendly alternatives and lab-grown meat.

—Ryan Roth, High School Ethics Bowler

Chapter 12

Ethics Bowl at San Quentin

Connie Krosney and Kathleen J. Richards

Hosting Ethics Bowl in prisons, an initiative that began over a decade ago, proved very successful, providing a rich and welcome experience for people who are incarcerated. The program at San Quentin, part of the curriculum of Mount Tamalpais College—whose campus is within the prison itself—has been taking place annually for several years. It has become an eye-opening experience for those inmates who take part, the college students who come for the event, and those who judge and moderate. This is another way Ethics Bowl thrives outside of academia, reinforcing the idea that "society is better off when all members, especially those who are marginalized, treat each other with respect and dignity."

* * *

One of the goals of Ethics Bowls is to take philosophy out of the realm of stuffy, professorial enclaves and into the broader public space. It is designed to apply philosophical and specifically ethical theories to real life events. Most often Bowls are held in schools—colleges, high schools, and middle schools. You may be surprised to learn that they also take place in prisons.

Prisons are dangerous places for many reasons, and those who are incarcerated must navigate prison rules and politics daily. This reality can be an impediment to engaging in academic pursuits, including taking college classes and participating in Ethics Bowls. Most view attending college as an uplifting and prosocial activity. Real-life events inside of a carceral institution can be quite different from those in the free (outside) community.

Despite these realities and complications, Ethics Bowl is alive and well at San Quentin State Prison.

INTRODUCING THE SAN QUENTIN ETHICS BOWL TEAM

Mount Tamalpais College (MTC) is a recently formed college whose only campus is inside San Quentin State Prison, located just north of San Francisco in Marin County, California. In response to students' requests for extracurricular activities to further hone critical thinking and writing skills, the school asked Kathy Richards, an English instructor, to help start a debate group. Coincidentally, at about the same time, Kyle Robertson from the Center for Public Policy approached MTC about the possibility of bringing the Ethics Bowl into the college program. Kyle and Kathy worked together to organize and coach the team, and the Ethics Bowl began during the fall semester in 2017 as a noncredit extracurricular activity. After attending the first match between University of California Santa Cruz and MTC, Connie Krosney, also an MTC faculty and board member, began coaching as well.

The MTC team has been comprised of twelve members, all men. Ranging in age from twenty-three to seventy, they come from a variety of backgrounds—African American, Latino, White, and Asian. Many have been incarcerated for over ten years, not uncommonly since they were teenagers, and many have indeterminate life sentences. They are all enrolled in or have graduated from MTC. One had earned an advanced degree prior to incarceration, others had some college before their incarceration, and still others enrolled in college for the first time during their incarceration. Because San Quentin has a level two (out of four) security designation, the general population tends to skew older. Many students have moved "up" from higher level security prisons, and quite a few have already served long sentences. To gain acceptance to MTC, students must successfully complete precollege courses in math and English, a robust challenge for people who have not been in school—much less a college class—for a long time. Those who have previous college experience can successfully pass an aptitude test to gain admittance.

The prerequisite for joining the team is successful completion of the first two English courses in the college program. All of the members have been involved in the self-help and personal growth groups omnipresent at San Quentin. They have been, for the most part, isolated from society, although they do watch television—especially sports—and have social interactions within the prison.

PREPARING FOR THE ETHICS BOWL

MTC team members have to prepare the way other college teams do. Although their life experience grants them certain advantages when preparing, they also work under unique handicaps. As one student wrote, "There were internal and external barriers that I had to navigate around, such as: an overall lack of experience with the Ethics Bowl, vast age differences, prison politics, self-limiting beliefs . . ."

We begin the term, as many other coaches do, by introducing the students to three ethical theories: deontology, utilitarianism, and virtue. We use Michael Sandel's excellent text, *Justice*, and articles as suggested in the case notes from the Ethics Bowl organization. Since there is no internet access and the prison library is limited, additional research resources are not readily available. We try to help the students to apply each theory to a case.

In academic settings, Ethics Bowl coaches work with students, often philosophy majors, who usually have almost limitless access to resources to further their education in philosophy and other disciplines. Access to online sources is taken for granted. The MTC team is composed mostly of people who have been out of the education system for years, sometimes decades. Some have never experienced using Google or any search engine. Others, who have some technological expertise, are frustrated by the limited internet accessibility in the prison.

This lack of access can also be a strength. Perhaps this absence of voluminous resources pushes San Quentin team members toward deeper reflection, encouraging them to use their own minds and those of their peers as resources. Each team member has access to the same articles and ideas about each case, so the positions they discuss may be more authentically their own. When they use the ethical theories to analyze their own and others' solutions, they may also be calling upon previous teachings, such as religious training, ethnic ethos, or family tradition, consciously or unconsciously.

Although they are always concerned with issues that affect them as incarcerated persons or that deal with police and criminal activity, they are also fascinated with social responsibility, environmental justice, individual and community rights and responsibilities, and religious freedom. In other words, although their experience is often quite limited, their minds and interests are open, curious, and far-reaching.

At first, like most Ethics Bowl participants, our students are quite tentative. They see issues in contrasting terms but are open to learning and thinking about more nuanced ways of approaching situations. They want to know more, to understand more, to understand the multiple perspectives of their peers. They are also eager to learn what their coaches think, but we actively attempt to turn the light back on to them. These older students bring their extensive life experiences to the classroom, which provide a wider lens through which to examine the issue at hand.

In fact, although it is intimidating for many of these students to experience being part of a team, they come to value this highly. They see what they learn as helpful in their everyday lives as well.

We think what makes the Ethics Bowl more conducive to a prison setting is that the format teaches one to practice consideration and to respectfully disagree with an opposing view. This minimizes the risk of confrontations arising.

As we meet regularly over several months, a sense of commitment to the team grows. Participation is entirely voluntary, and the members are appreciative of each other as they contribute. We have seen good friendships form as a result.

CHALLENGES OF PREPARATION

As substantial as these challenges are, the larger challenge is introducing the idea of dialogue. During Ethics Bowls, team members are encouraged to talk openly and honestly about difficult and complex issues. But in a carceral setting, honestly expressing one's views on controversial topics can be fraught with peril. This is especially true when discussing the humanities, discussions during which social conditions are recognized, dissected, and discussed. MTC team members are often nervous speaking their minds. They also work hard to not assume that one knows the position of another. They strive to avoid conflict since in prison, conflict and disagreement have led to serious outcomes for these men. As they struggle to rehabilitate themselves so that they may one day be released, they have often been advised to "walk away" from conflict—in order to survive.

Learning to work as a team, in which one member speaks for others at times, can also prove uncomfortable for these students. One source of conflict may be that an individual feels demeaned or diminished by someone else speaking for him. As one team member wrote, "The vast majority of the incarcerated cannot distinguish between a 'different opinion' and disrespect; therefore, they tend to settle such with violence."

Perhaps most significantly, the very idea of competing is initially somewhat threatening to some students. As a rule, in carceral settings, teams or groups of any kind are discouraged because of the threats of gangs and/or violence. In our meetings with the team, we emphasize the importance of dialogue, which incorporates active listening and reflection. Learning to engage in dialogue means learning to engage in healthy disagreement, without disrespect.

There is tension, but it is positive tension, stimulating and affirming. As one team member said,

> The best part of participating in the Ethics Bowl was spending time together with the coaches and the other men, collaborating as a team. Despite being surrounded by hundreds of other people . . . incarceration is a lonely experience. I am convinced that working together as a team, toward a common goal, is a valuable, and a needed experience for those incarcerated.

MEETING TEAMS FROM THE "OUTSIDE"

Ethics Bowl affords our students the chance to engage in true intellectual and friendly exchanges with students from other colleges; it is also a rare opportunity to engage with and experience the outside world. The MTC students take pride finding themselves in matches with students from elite institutions. Our main match has been with teams from the University of California, Santa Cruz (UCSC). However, teams from San Jose State University and Stanford University have come to San Quentin for our practice matches.

One scrimmage was highly memorable. The case involved voting rights for felons. Most states either restrict or strip convicted felons of their right to vote during incarceration and, usually, through the parole period as well. In California, after discharge from parole, voting rights are automatically restored; in other states, a person discharged from parole needs to personally petition the governor for restoration of voting rights. Only Maine and Vermont permit people to vote during their entire incarceration.

The MTC team met with an Ethics Bowl team from a Bay Area university, comprised of students in their first and second years. The Bay Area university team took the position that incarcerated people should not be stripped of their right to vote, in part because voting is a basic right of citizens and that right should never be taken away except in extreme cases, such as treason, a crime against the government itself. Their presentation included a proposal for a carceral system that strictly tailored consequences for breaking the social contract to the specific offense.

Here's what a member of the MTC team replied: "My commitment offense involved a man losing his life; that man's voice is no longer heard in the public sphere, including in the voting booth, so why should I have the right to voice my opinion?"

Real-life events, indeed, and a powerful moment for both teams.

LEARNING AND TEACHING TOGETHER

Most, if not all, believe that offering Ethics Bowl in a carceral setting benefits incarcerated participants as well as nonincarcerated participants. What the MTC team members take away from engaging in Ethics Bowl is profound. The team members themselves report that participation in Ethics Bowl "greatly enhanced critical thinking skills," especially through the shared preparation and dialogue; that is, by listening to each other and being open to different ideas.

MTC team members find themselves participating in an activity totally unrelated to their incarceration. They wrestle with important ethical questions that affect society as a whole, not just those inside prison walls. Even more, the fact that they are viewed as worthy participants by faculty and students from outside higher education institutions affirms and sometimes surprises them. This is understandable when we consider that every day they receive implicit and explicit messages that they are "less than human" and that their lives don't matter. When, in Ethics Bowl, they experience their ideas being heard and as having value, they begin to see themselves as valued and worthy of respect, and as potential contributors to the society. Team members are also surprised and gratified by the interest shown by "the Yard"—other incarcerated people, especially other MTC students—who show up for the scrimmages and matches.

The MTC team also realizes that they have an opportunity to dispel the various negative attitudes and stereotypical images of incarcerated people that most people on the outside harbor. As the team knows well, many people on the outside have never seen the inside of a prison and have created impressions and ideas about the people who reside there, often derived from television and movies. Bringing free people into a carceral institution to directly interact with the people who live there affords free people an opportunity to experience the humanity—the complexity—of incarcerated people.

Visiting teams also benefit. We have been told by visiting team members and their coaches that coming to San Quentin and participating in Ethics Bowl has been eye-opening, even life-changing, at least for some. One graduating college student told us that she intended to move to the area, in part so that she could teach in our college program at the prison. This reaction isn't surprising when you consider that not only does our society lock people away but it also locks away the thoughts of those incarcerated. When many of us on the outside see incarcerated people in a positive format like Ethics Bowl, our minds tend to open, allowing us to reconsider the stereotypes we've grown up with, and to see people who are incarcerated as human beings worthy of consideration and respect.

In these ways, both teams, those outside and inside, hold up mirrors to each other, and their perceptions of each other change as their understanding of each other's capacities grows more expansive. Positive interactions between the free and incarcerated communities enhance rehabilitation for the incarcerated and enhance the free community's understanding of the criminal justice system and those caught up in it. As one MTC team member wrote:

> The best part . . . is the positive exposure of incarcerated people to those in free society. College students—who will be tomorrow's leaders—can see firsthand the societal benefits of providing a college education in state prisons.

ETHICS BOWL DAY: MTC AND UC SANTA CRUZ

The 2017–2018 San Quentin Ethics Bowl team met the team from UC Santa Cruz in February 2018. Both teams showed up nervous. As spectators from inside and outside began to arrive at the venue, the Santa Cruz students huddled outside the chapel, where the match was to be held. When the MTC team arrived, they approached the other team to introduce themselves. That broke the ice. Both teams admitted that they were intimidated by the perceived strengths of the other: the MTC team was sure that the UC Santa Cruz team would be much smarter than they were, and the UC Santa Cruz team was equally sure that the San Quentin team would be composed of scary guys. Sharing this moment of reciprocal recognition and a good laugh, they walked together into the chapel.

One of the cases that day was about the so-called Goldwater Rule, a rule prohibiting psychologists from opining about the mental health of living public figures. The case cited the turmoil arising from the fact that mental health professionals were offering opinions about then-president Trump's mental fitness to serve, without having personally examined or interacted with him.

The UCSC team's presentation focused on the public's right to know whether the person running for or holding the office of President of the United States is mentally fit. They argued that all candidates for this very important office should submit to a mental health examination. The MTC team focused on the stigma associated with mental health. In particular, they worried that labeling Trump as mentally ill would do a disservice to those many people who function perfectly well in society while dealing with mental health issues. The team also espoused the belief that labeling his behaviors as those of someone mentally ill would ultimately serve to excuse his conduct. Many, if not most, of those who are incarcerated suffer from trauma, usually multiple traumas. This is an example of how their life experience gave the MTC team a different lens with which to examine the case.

After the event, Amy Jamgochian, Chief Academic Officer at MTC, reflected on the value that Ethics Bowl brings to MTC students:

> I hadn't heard of the Ethics Bowl format before Kyle [Kyle Robertson of the Center for Public Philosophy] introduced it to us, and I love it. It offers components of argumentation that are missing in traditional debate and that create a more nuanced and thoughtful dialogue. I'm delighted that our students have the chance to be exposed to this format. We aim to offer a college experience inside prison that is as close to college outside prison as possible. This means that our courses are rigorous, and we have high expectations of our students, but we're also trying to build a campus community, which the event played a lovely role in. Our students are humans embedded in communities, whether they leave prison in a week, in a year, or never. They have cellmates, friends, wives, mothers, children, grandchildren, and friends. They write op-eds, short stories, novels, and letters to senators. They teach courses to other incarcerated people, and they advocate for themselves and for their friends and families. It may well be the goal of the prison system to strip incarcerated people of citizenship, but humanity can't be squelched, and there are modes of citizenship that don't require voting or physical freedom. The principles of Ethics Bowl are the principles of healthy democracy: understanding the issues, advocating for one's beliefs, listening to others' ideas, and engaging in respectful dialogue.

Ethics Bowls in prisons are positive models of what is possible when people from many different walks of life engage in thoughtful dialogue about important issues of our day. They reinforce that society is better off when all members, especially those who are marginalized, treat each other with respect and dignity.

They also allow everyone involved to see that incarcerated people are not one-dimensional and that they are not defined by their crime, as Bryan Stevenson of the Equal Justice Initiative has so eloquently argued. These positive experiences help to reinforce that there may be welcome mats and opportunities out in the free community after release.

All of us, incarcerated or free, are complex. We all would be better served to shed our stereotypes and preconceived notions of each other. How better to accomplish this than by talking together.

* * *

> I participated in the Ethics Bowl for two years (2016, 2017). My experience there taught me two invaluable lessons. First, I learned to think for myself and arrive at my own conclusions from principled reasoning.

Second, Ethics Bowl taught me to think and operate in spaces of high uncertainty, where many things may not be well-defined. Overall, these two lessons have bolstered my confidence and conviction in my judgment, especially when pursuing less conventional paths or projects. I have found the skills I learned through Ethics Bowl transferable to much of my current work in computer science, whether it be in designing complex software libraries or communicating with others and working on a larger team. I would highly recommend any student who has the ability and interest to participate in Ethics Bowl to get involved in a heartbeat!

—Adam Pahlavi, High School Ethics Bowl alumnus

Chapter 13

Meeting the Challenge
The Future of Ethics Bowl

Alex M. Richardson

What does the future hold for Ethics Bowl? Alex Richardson reflects on this question as he recounts the innovations that have marked Ethics Bowl from its beginnings as an intercollegiate event to recent events in high schools, middle schools, and retirement facilities. Richardson mentions an increasing array of innovative resources and organizations devoted to propagating Ethics Bowl events, skills, and civil discussions for all levels of ability and competition venues. He also sees Ethics Bowl as a progressive, case-based, deliberative pedagogy that delves into alternate approaches to ethical instruction. The future of Ethics Bowl, says Richardson, will continue with enhanced technological access to events and a focus on greater inclusion and equity.

* * *

> There has never been an experience or a greater tool that has made me believe not only that I can be a better person but that I can challenge the world to be better and that there is that possibility . . . There's [sic] so many things that get lost in the politics and the negative side of the world, but [Ethics Bowl] gives you a genuine platform to challenge the world to be better, and I think that's really special.—Student participant, National High School Ethics Bowl

As previous chapters have demonstrated, the Ethics Bowl discussion format and Ethics Bowl programs across the United States (and increasingly, across the world) present and model a better way to argue for the tens of thousands of participants they serve.[1] This remarkable activity inculcates individual habits of mind and norms of cooperation and deliberation that are crucial to a healthily functioning society. By creating constructive spaces for students to think, talk, and work together—even and especially over stark disagreement about their fundamental beliefs—the Ethics Bowl provides fertile ground from which the inheritors of American democracy will spring.

The activity does this important work at a time when the bonds of moral and civic community are strained by a once-in-a-century pandemic and related social crises and a moral reckoning over questions of race, identity, and belonging. An often "scorched earth" political climate is fueled by antipathy, motivated reasoning, and the pernicious assumption that disagreements about values must reduce to partisan rhetorical conflict. This climate, in many ways, encourages us to think of our fellow citizens not as well-meaning contributors to the shared project of democracy but as enemy combatants who must be defeated.

In these circumstances, virtues like open-mindedness, reciprocity, humility, and civility are more important than ever. With these important values in view, important next steps include expanding reach and impact, ensuring universal access for participants, and adapting the format for new audiences and use cases (some of which are detailed in this volume). This chapter highlights several new tools and approaches to pursue these goals. Ultimately, we hope and intend to bring about a future for the Ethics Bowl that will provide students of all ages with a collaborative, meaningful, and deeply transformative experience in moral and civic education.

GROWING THE ETHICS BOWL COMMUNITY

The Ethics Bowl activity has grown dramatically during its lifetime. Since its creation in the 1990s by Robert Ladenson, the Association for Practical and Professional Ethics Intercollegiate Ethics Bowl (APPE IEB) has grown to serve nearly one thousand students from 114 universities across the United States.[2] More recently it expanded to serve students at two-year institutions. The National High School Ethics Bowl (NHSEB), founded in 2012 by the Parr Center for Ethics and the Squire Family Foundation, has grown from serving around a thousand students in eleven states to serving nearly four thousand across thirty-two states in just under a decade.[3] These students come from over three hundred schools, public and private. NHSEB has also consulted on the design and early implementation of Ethics Bowl programs for high school students in half a dozen countries as of mid-2021.

Since the Ethics Bowl depends on large-scale face-to-face interactions among participants, and, at higher levels of competition, substantial travel distance, the onset of the COVID-19 pandemic in early 2020 presented both major challenges and clear opportunities for all organizations involved. Both NHSEB and APPE IEB moved quickly to preserve all participants know and love about the activity (and to invest in its future) by creating the possibility for fully virtual Ethics Bowls for the first time in history. APPE IEB has built on existing video conferencing tools to great effect, and NHSEB's administration has designed and developed a new and innovative online competition and administration platform.[4]

As the world recovers from the pandemic, the Ethics Bowl community has begun to incorporate elements of its emergency response into its format and operations more generally. NHSEB is currently developing the capacity to bring the option for online and hybrid-format Ethics Bowl matches to its community at scale in both competitive and classroom/curricular use cases, and APPE IEB continues to retain pandemic-prompted flexibility with an option for fully online regional bowls and an innovative online bowl with an asynchronous discussion format.

These promising innovations will increase and augment the activity's reach and impact—both in terms of providing new and experimental venues for discussion and by significantly improving the participant and volunteer experience of existing Ethics Bowl programs in new and innovative ways.

ETHICS BOWL FOR ALL: EXPANDING ACCESS AND INCLUSION

However, the rapid expansion of the Ethics Bowl has not always been evenly distributed across geographic areas or demographics. Students from private and well-resourced public schools, for example, tend to be overrepresented in the activity compared to their representation in the general population. This is true for at least two reasons: (1) students from those schools are more likely to benefit from established co- and extracurricular programming at their schools, and (2) students from those schools often perform better in individual Ethics Bowl events, for many reasons. Well-resourced schools have outsized capacity for clubs and activities and devote particular attention to those with demonstrable academic benefits for their students. Furthermore, students at well-resourced schools are more likely to have received dedicated instruction on critical thinking, philosophy, or moral theory, which then helps them excel at Ethics Bowl. Students and teachers from communities and schools with less access to resources often struggle to get extracurricular programs like the Ethics Bowl off the ground.

To lower barriers to entry for students and teachers, NHSEB has recently launched a new pilot program—NHSEBBridge. This online-first Ethics Bowl for schools new to the activity specifically targets underserved communities and underresourced schools that may not otherwise have access to the program's benefits.[5] NHSEBBridge is integrated with an experiential learning course in the Philosophy Department at UNC-Chapel Hill in which undergraduates provide coaching, instruction on moral reasoning, and helpful feedback to participants.

Beyond these centralized efforts, regional Ethics Bowls, too, are implementing promising access and equity initiatives.[6] APPE IEB has also made promising inroads with students from underrepresented groups by expanding their recently created Two-Year College Qualifying Regional and conducting targeted outreach with historically black colleges and universities across the country. Though in its early stages, this work is crucial to expanding the Ethics Bowl community in a sustainable and inclusive way and making good on the goal of comprehensive access for student participants.

As the activity has grown over the past several years, its deep meaningfulness to students has become increasingly clear. In addition to some promising early quantitative data on skills development, students report that they often think of the Ethics Bowl as an empowering and transformative experience. As one high school student participating in the NHSEB commented:

> The Ethics Bowl competition allows for students to have a safe space to speak about real issues that are often too sensitive for a classroom environment. Ethics Bowl allows students to openly speak out and work as a team to effectively find the best solution for everyone involved.

The kinds of learning that the Ethics Bowl promotes is referred to as *deliberative pedagogy*[7]—the collaborative process of thinking through cases together and the process of crafting affirmative arguments or critical and responsive commentaries[8] on views different from their own. Increasingly this happens before students arrive at their local Ethics Bowl. Thus, an important future goal for the activity should also be to take this learning process seriously and pay careful attention to shaping and modeling Ethics Bowl pedagogy done well.

NHSEB has begun to do this by launching NHSEBAcademy—a new online space for student, teacher, and volunteer learning about and around the Ethics Bowl. It includes a growing library of resources in various formats (print, graphic, video, and interactives), an innovative program called "the Studio," which allows students around the country to book on-demand appointments with NHSEB experts and staffers for coaching assistance, "ethical toolkit" discussions, argument workshops, and so forth, and a new series of real-time online experiences, NHSEBAcademy Live. Taken together, these resources emphasize an accessible, common-language approach using a conceptual and methodological toolkit that does not necessarily reduce to explicit moral theory instruction.

APPE IEB has also begun to pay increased attention to pedagogical development around the Ethics Bowl in its Summer Workshop series—which feature sessions on teaching with deliberative pedagogy, diversifying the activity and surrounding community, and more.

This focus on deliberative pedagogy alongside the Ethics Bowl event structure helps students navigate complex issues in the context of their various communities in ways informed by tolerance for each other and diverse perspectives, patience, and self-restraint.[9] Beyond modeling and fostering these key democratic virtues, deliberative pedagogy can begin to prompt a particular kind of empowerment for students belonging to underrepresented or oppressed groups and instill humility and empathy among students who are comparatively dominantly situated.

Students report feeling more confidence in themselves, their own value judgments, and their own agency. One student explains that Ethics Bowl provides a venue to discuss issues they cared about "and actually be listened to." Another explained that before participating, they often felt powerless and that their views on important social or political issues were treated dismissively; however, Ethics Bowl is "such a great environment to speak out and share what you know, because finally I'm not silenced from speaking out about these topics." Still another student launched a club for community members:

> The school doesn't encourage talking about political topics, however when those have effected [sic] my community so much, it has become more important to talk about it. Without Ethics Bowl, I wouldn't have had enough courage to speak out about these topics.[10]

Deliberative, case-based pedagogy focuses on the substantive equality of students and their dialogical contributions. It also helps them navigate their moral and political worlds more effectively and empathetically. The approach here is similar to an approach to classroom pedagogy advanced by Anthony Laden, who emphasizes "skills like listening to others, understanding them and allowing their words to matter, as well as, when appropriate, being able to trust others, which may require openness to being vulnerable to them."[11]

Although Ethics Bowl is in its adolescence and provisional early data is compelling, there is a dearth of rigorous educational research about its impact in the long and short term. Are students attaining and retaining the skills, values, and norms Ethics Bowl can impart? Longitudinal studies are needed, as well as carefully designed tools to assess and evaluate the ways in which the deliberative approach at the heart of Ethics Bowl is successful. This will involve securing financial and operational support for a suitably comprehensive multisite and multilevel study of the Ethics Bowl as it exists today.

DIALOGUE ACROSS THE LIFESPAN: NEW VENUES FOR ETHICS BOWL PEDAGOGY

Given the democratic import of the deliberative model so central to Ethics Bowl, and the activity's successes thus far, there is great promise for its future expansion and extension to other venues and use cases. For example, if students in schools and colleges enjoy and appreciate Ethics Bowl as an extracurricular activity, why not include it in the curriculum and import it into the classroom? Important inroads are being made: middle schools in Texas, high schools in North Carolina, and undergraduate courses across the country are being designed to prepare students for participation in APPE IEB.

In other words, Ethics Bowl is catching on as a distinctive classroom pedagogy as well.[12] Early work from the Squire Family Foundation and the Philosophy Learning and Teaching Organization (PLATO) outlined a model for including deliberative pedagogy into grade school classrooms,[13] and the Parr Center for Ethics is currently piloting a classroom integration program that pairs specially selected Ethics Bowl cases with core concepts, texts, and performance standards. This program also features an adjusted classroom discussion format and written and verbal activities for students; it has the capability to link classrooms across states and regions making use of the groundwork laid by the NHSEBOne Ethics Bowl platform.

In addition to expanding into classrooms, the format and pedagogical core of the Ethics Bowl lends itself well to working with other audiences as well. As of 2019, a growing set of programs in California, Oregon, and New Jersey—supported by the Squire Family Foundation—brings Ethics Bowl to middle school students using a developmentally appropriate discussion format and approach to case writing. Pilot programs in the Philosophy Outreach Program at the University of North Carolina and elsewhere use Ethics Bowl cases and methods as the basis for discussion groups among retired seniors, and the Parr Center for Ethics plans to host the first Intergenerational Ethics Bowl, between retirees and high school students participating in NHSEB, in 2022.

Many organizations have begun to experiment with importing deliberative pedagogy to workplaces via Ethics Bowl. At the organization's 2021 International Conference, the APPE Board of Directors piloted a Corporate Ethics Bowl discussion among ethics and compliance leaders in the private sector. In North Carolina, the Parr Center for Ethics has pilots in progress with local government leaders in Chapel Hill and Durham and has used

Ethics Bowl pedagogy to design training and professional development initiatives for the Human Resources department at UNC-Chapel Hill. These experiments are in their early days but offer exciting glimpses into future adaptations and applications of the Ethics Bowl format.

The future of the Ethics Bowl, then, is one of much promise, though much work remains to make it all it can be. This chapter has outlined some key areas in which focused attention, support, and work would greatly improve (and is in fact already improving) the activity. We are making strides in terms of expansion toward ubiquity and equal access through innovative programming, expanding and evaluating its pedagogical goals and associated participant outcomes, and bringing a deliberative model of learning and collaboration to new venues.

Thanks to these efforts, the Ethics Bowl can live up to its stated ideals of promoting those norms and virtues so central to democratic citizenship which are needed now more than ever. Properly expanded and studied, our activity will empower and challenge its participants to learn, work, live, and ultimately flourish as more thoughtful and engaged members of the complex moral and political communities to which they belong.

[See references for this chapter in the References and Resources section.]

* * *

Participating in the Ethics Bowl was one of the best decisions I made as a student. Before joining the Ethics team, I was at a crossroads in terms of my education. In that moment, I had no idea how impactful and important the Bowl would be to me and my journey. Ethics Bowl gave me confidence in my future. I was a part of something bigger than myself. I wanted to do better and reach higher than I ever had before. This Bowl and the people that I met while participating changed the trajectory of my life in a bright and beautiful way.

—Austin Duncan, Intercollegiate Ethics Bowl alumnus

Chapter 14

From Ethics Bowler to Coach
Lifelong Learning through Ethics Bowl

Rachel Robison-Greene

How does Ethics Bowl contribute to lifelong learning? Rachel Robison-Greene recounts her initiation into Ethics Bowl as a winning undergraduate competitor with life-changing experiences, both intellectual and social. She has taken on a range of roles—team member, coach, judge, and mentor—as she advanced from student to professor. Not only does she regard Ethics Bowl as an effective pedagogy that enables students to enrich their viewpoints of ethical issues, to learn to listen, and to be heard but it also helped her develop compassion for others. As Rachel knows firsthand, students who participate in Ethics Bowl remember it as a high point of their undergraduate experience, initiating a trajectory that leads them to continue their quest for ethical understanding and to widen their perceptions of the world.

* * *

In the fall of 2002, I sat around a table with four friends, talking about Dance Safe—a program that provided free drug testing at raves. The program was designed to prevent people from seriously hurting themselves or dying by taking drugs cut with harmful chemicals. Yet because the five of us were on an Ethics Bowl team, we were tasked with deciding whether the Dance Safe mission was ethically defensible.

Many of the students in that particular state commuter college came from a wide variety of backgrounds and were "nontraditional." Two of the students on the team, for example, were more than ten years older than typical college students: one had been in the military, and another had taken a long hiatus for personal reasons. I was a freshman in college and had been raised in a conservative area. My experience with the world was, as one might expect, *extremely* limited. Up to that point, I had never been around drugs or drug users—at least, as far as I knew.

At the first practice session, I shared that I had been up late the night before, preparing my position on all fifteen cases that would be discussed at the Ethics Bowl, including the Dance Safe case. We had planned on discussing all of the cases that afternoon but ended up sitting together for hours discussing just Dance Safe. My position was that no one should ever do anything to contribute to breaking the law ever, under any circumstances.

I still smile when I think back on this because now it seems to me so wrongheaded, and boy, were my teammates—all of whom came from very different backgrounds and had more experience with the topic than I did— ready and eager to tell me so. By the end of the night, I had totally changed my thinking about drugs and drug testing after listening to the stories and arguments that my teammates shared.

As my philosophical education progressed, I would read philosophers who theorized about ethics as a social endeavor. I would consider positions that defined the ethical community as a group of individuals who offer, evaluate, and accept or reject reasons. But well before I engaged with those ideas in a formal, philosophical way, I dove right in and experienced them through participating in the Ethics Bowl.

FROM BOWLER TO COACH

Nearly twenty years later, I am a philosophy professor and long-standing coach of an Ethics Bowl team. Leading our prep sessions, I emphasize with my students that I want our practices to be a safe place where they can explore a wide range of ideas and perspectives. Sometimes it irritates them when one teammate holds out on endorsing the group's position on a case. I tell them that, once upon a time, I was the holdout and that the discussions of Dance Safe changed my worldview. I encourage my students to value the difficult discussions during Ethics Bowl prep because they provide us with meaningful opportunities for both individual and group growth. The social endeavor of responding to reasons makes us better reasoners as individuals and makes us more virtuous people.

Preparing for and participating in Ethics Bowl also emphasizes the importance of empathy when engaging in ethical reasoning and decision-making. Interacting with team members, Ethics Bowlers learn to not only analyze the cases, but also to be confronted with counterfactuals that expand our circles of ethical regard and make us aware of the wide variety of people and living beings with whom we live. Ethics Bowl prep allows us to imagine situations in which we will likely never be involved. By flexing our ethical muscles, we can project ourselves into those situations we couldn't have imagined.

RELEVANCE ACROSS THE DECADES

I was an Ethics Bowl team member in the immediate aftermath of the terrorist attacks on 9/11. The news was nonstop; every television showed footage on a seemingly endless loop. There were countless commentaries about the "war on terror." As a result, many of us carried around mental photos of the perpetrators. The dominant narrative, a narrative in which many of us readily and eagerly participated, was that we were living through a time during which Americans came together in grief. Despite our differences, we united in defiance of a common enemy.

Shortly thereafter, I took my first plane ride as an adult to California for an Ethics Bowl tournament. The intensity on the security lines frightened me, and my coach told me that they were newly installed, a measure taken in the aftermath of the attacks.

One of the cases we had to present during the Bowl was about racial profiling at airports. We had talked about this case during practice, but engaging with the other team during the round itself elevated my thinking, especially after my experiences getting on the plane. I felt my ethical circle expand, recalling how I had felt going through the airport checkpoint, and could imagine what a person of color might experience going through the same process, especially if that person was from the Middle East or looked like someone who did. When I returned home, I consumed news differently. I was more critical of the coverage, and found myself able to consider how people from other countries might respond to the ways in which the news was reported.

Many Ethics Bowlers have similar transformative experiences. And many coaches have seen our students' ability to empathize grow. We witness very young students, just out of high school, seriously grapple with policies that impact the elderly—a group to which the very young often do not give much thought. We hear about students who have become vegetarians or vegans after preparing cases related to the plight of nonhuman animals.

During the 2020–2021 Ethics Bowl season, our hearts ached as we watched students grapple with the COVID-19 pandemic. As I had been grateful for Ethics Bowl after the attack on the World Trade Center, they were grateful for the Ethics Bowl because it helped them work through their thoughts and feelings about COVID-19. Cases asked them to engage with many issues in addition to the pandemic: the deaths of Black people at the hands of the police; the resultant demonstrations demanding justice; and the threats to the stability of our democracy.

They learned to imagine how others might experience the same circumstances they found themselves in. What was it like, for instance, to be a grandmother dying alone, unable to see her children and grandchildren to say goodbye? How did nurses working in COVID wards feel? How did they deal with their concerns that they might contract the deadly virus and pass it along to their immunocompromised partner or child? What thoughts run through your mind if you're a young man of color pulled over for driving when you know you weren't speeding, or parents waiting up all night for a child who will not be coming home?

No one can perfectly project themselves into someone else's consciousness. We can't fully know what it is like to be another person; we're trapped in our own subjective experience of the world. That said, we can't make sound ethical judgments unless we really take time to consider and understand, to the best of our ability, the concerns and interests of other living beings. Whatever position Ethics Bowlers assume when analyzing cases, if the Ethics Bowl has worked its magic, they learn to arrive at that position by engaging with the ethical scenario through the lens of empathy and compassion. This is one of the primary goals of the activity and one of the skills students are equipped with as a result of their participation.

Not all students who participate in the Ethics Bowl are philosophy majors, but all who participate are doing philosophy. As a professor, I often tell my students that there is no view or set of views they should feel ready to adopt at the end of the semester. The goal is to become more introspective and to check their own views for internal coherence. Coherence alone is not enough to establish truth—some coherent world views can be wacky and entirely unhinged from reality—but if students introspect and find that their beliefs don't cohere, they should recognize this as a call for further reflection. In other words, training for Ethics Bowl helps us all sharpen our skills when it comes to checking our beliefs for coherence.

Of course, from a competitive standpoint, there is no reason why a team's position on two different cases must be coherent. When judging is done right, each case exists in isolation. From a pedagogical point of view, however, it is useful for coaches to point out the coherence or lack thereof between the team's positions on cases. For example, why might a team defend a family's right to keep their loved one alive on a ventilator on the grounds that all life has inherent value but then go on to support the execution of an incarcerated person in another case and experimenting on nonhuman animals in yet another?

Participation in the Ethics Bowl provides students with the opportunity to not only practice applying ethical principles, but also to evaluate their reasons or lack of reasons for applying those principles in some circumstances but not in others. In other words, it equips them with sharpened skills when it comes to checking beliefs for coherence.

CHANNELING COMPETITIVE FEELINGS

I was fiercely competitive as a young woman, as are many of our students. I behaved very badly on several occasions—complaining loudly about the way a round had been judged, not realizing until my teammates alerted me to the fact that the judges I was vehemently criticizing were walking behind us, within earshot. Another time I skipped watching the championship round because our team had lost a match we should have won. Fortunately, coaches know how to handle petulant behavior like this, taking team members aside and reminding them that winning is nice but isn't the point. Most coaches realize that we need to channel our urge to win into constructive channels so the competitive aspect of Ethics Bowl doesn't derail us from appreciating its true value.

Now that I'm on the other side, I realize that winning rounds or tournaments is the very least important part of Ethics Bowl. The students who really capture the spirit of the Ethics Bowl learn to be gracious losers. They remain curious about the perspectives of other participants, even when those participants have just beaten them handily in a round.

EXPANDING THE REACH OF ETHICS BOWL

Many members of the Ethics Bowl community have recognized the value that the Ethics Bowl has for a much wider audience than traditional American college students. In recent years, as the collegiate Ethics Bowl has grown, we've also seen the rapid expansion of the National High School Ethics Bowl and the recent launch of the National Middle School Ethics Bowl. I have helped train Ethics Bowl high school and middle school students in Australia, China, and Thailand. In partnership with others, I've been part of initiatives to bring Ethics Bowl into prisons. People are working diligently in similar ways across the globe. These efforts underscore the reality that deliberate and principled reasoning is a tool to which we all have access.

This realization is important in terms of teaching in general. Let's face it: most students won't remember the three main objections to cultural ethical relativism or the difference Aristotle draws between the vegetative and the animate souls. We have to make peace with this. But when we use Ethics Bowl in the classroom, it accomplishes what a good college education is supposed to accomplish—it creates lifelong learners. There will be exceptions, but for the most part, students who participate in Ethics Bowl put themselves in an excellent position to become and remain curious, compassionate, and open minded; in short, they have the skills and desire to seek out answers to important questions.

Over the years, students have told me that Ethics Bowl was the best learning experience of their lives. Recently, one of my students gave a speech at the Ethics Bowl Summer Workshop in which he described how Ethics Bowl helped him recover from addiction and discover new meaning in his life. Many of us who have helped Ethics Bowl grow and thrive have similar stories.

We live in turbulent and confrontational times marked by a lack of understanding and compassion. Anyone reading this who is in a position to start an Ethics Bowl program, please do so. It will contribute, even if just a little, to bringing about the kind of world in which we would all like to live.

* * *

The best part of Ethics Bowl is its applicability to the real world. Every day, there are countless decisions we have to make—some trivial, some important. I have found that my experiences in Ethics Bowl have allowed me to approach difficult situations with an open mind and a greater willingness to listen to others. Ethics Bowl does not only involve speaking; listening is an equally critical, if not even more important, component.

—Han Byur (Hailee) Youn, High School Ethics Bowler

Appendix: Sample High School Ethics Bowl Case and Study Questions

NONHUMAN ANIMALS IN BIOMEDICAL RESEARCH

Biomedical experiments often rely on the use of nonhuman animals as test subjects. This research sometimes leads to important medical and scientific advances, but it also often exposes research subjects to disease, injury, and/or death without the possibility of consent, and without the promise that this research will be used to benefit nonhuman animal populations.

There are many examples of nonhuman subjects experiments that seem to have led to important medical and scientific breakthroughs. For example, experimental surgery conducted on the brains of monkeys led researchers to discover a new treatment for Parkinson's disease, which has now helped as many as 200,000 humans to greatly increase their quality of life. Granted, this kind of research can sometimes lead us astray as well, due to differences between human and nonhuman bodies. And at least some of the progress that we have made as a result of this kind of research might have occurred either way. Still, it is plausible that nonhuman subjects research has done substantial good for humans.

However, there are also many risks and harms that researchers impose on nonhuman subjects that they would never impose on human subjects (even if those humans were cognitively relevantly similar to nonhumans). For instance, in 1987 Mortimer Mishkin and Tim Appenzeller lesioned the brains of monkeys in order to learn how different structures in the brain contribute to forming memories. They did learn new information about memory in the process. However, this study left its research subjects neurologically impaired and unable to form memories. And this outcome is not at all uncommon: The vast majority of nonhuman subjects experience disease, injury, and/or death as a result of their involvement in biomedical research.

Currently in the United States, the Animal Welfare Act requires all federally funded research facilities that conduct animal research to have an Institutional Animal Care and Use Committee (IACUC). These committees review all research proposals that would use animal models and conduct inspections in research facilities. In particular, IACUCs aim to ensure that researchers use animal models only in worthwhile experiments, that researchers use animal models only when alternatives are unavailable, and that when researchers do use animal models, they avoid causing unnecessary harm (though in practice, many IACUCs treat these criteria as compatible with imposing disease, injury, and/or death on nonhuman subjects since they see these harms as a necessary part of worthwhile experiments).

However, critics of animal research claim that we need to do more in order to treat nonhuman subjects ethically. In particular, some animal rights advocates argue that we should perform experiments on nonhumans only if we would be willing to perform these experiments on cognitively relevantly similar humans (for example infants or severely cognitively disabled humans) as well. And of course, in the human case, most people believe that we should never knowingly and willingly inflict impairment or death on research subjects without the possibility of consent, no matter what we might learn as a result. In these cases, most people think, these harms are simply too high a price to pay.

Study Questions

1. How should we compare the value of scientific knowledge with the well-being of research subjects?
2. Are we justified in treating nonhuman subjects differently than cognitively relevantly similar human subjects? Why or why not?
3. Are we justified in treating some nonhuman subjects, such as primates, differently than others, such as mice? Why or why not?

This case was developed by the National High School Ethics Bowl, based at UNC's Parr Center for Ethics, and was included in the 2017 National Case Set.

Notes

CHAPTER 2

1. For an excellent and accessible book addressing this way of thinking about argument in detail, see Scott F. Aikin and Robert B. Talisse's *Why We Argue (And How We Should): A Guide to Political Disagreement in an Age of Unreason*, 2nd ed. (Routledge, 2019).
2. See David Perkins, "Learning to Reason: The Influence of Instruction, Prompts and Scaffolding, Metacognitive Knowledge, and General Intelligence on Informal Reasoning about Everyday Social and Political Issues," *Judgment and Decision Making* 14, no. 6 (Nov. 2019): 624–43.
3. See Ziva Kunda, "The Case for Motivated Reasoning," *Psychological Bulletin*, 108, no. 3 (1990): 480–98.
4. For an accessible article covering the basic idea, see David Robson, "Why Smart People Are More Likely To Believe Fake News," *The Guardian*, April 1, 2019.
5. For an excellent and accessible book-length discussion of cognitive dissonance from which I take this example, see Carol Tavris and Elliot Aronson, *Mistakes Were Made (But Not By Me)* (HMH Books, 2020).
6. The classic first line of "Can a good lawyer be a good person?" opens Charles Fried's article "The Lawyer as Friend: The Moral Foundations of the Lawyer-Client Relation," *Yale Law Journal* 85 (1976).

CHAPTER 4

1. Mary Flanagan and Helen Nissenbaum, *Values at Play in Digital Games* (Cambridge, MA: The MIT Press, 2016), 8–10. In addition, chapter 3 includes fifteen game elements. For the Bowl examination, we used only four of them. Chapter 3 is entitled "Game Elements: The Language of Values" and includes a third author, Jonathan Belman.

2. Robin Kramer, "Our Psychological Biases Mean Order Matters When We Judge Items in Sequence," *theconversation.com*, 2017, https://theconversation.com/our-psychological-biases-mean-order-matters-when-we-judge-items-in-sequence-70942 (accessed May 14, 2021); and Inga Wolframm, "Natural Bias the Hidden Controversy in Judging Sports," *Eurodressage.com*, 2010, https://www.eurodressage.com/2010/11/04/natural-bias-hidden-controversy-judging-sports (accessed May 14, 2021).

CHAPTER 11

1. Plato, *Plato: Laws 1 and 2*, trans. with commentary by Susan Sauvé Meyer (Oxford University Press, 2015).
2. Matthew Lipman, *Thinking in Education* (Cambridge: Cambridge University Press, 1991).
3. Walter C. Parker and Diana Hess, "Teaching with and for Discussion," *Teaching and Teacher Education* 17, no. 3 (2001): 273–89.
4. Diana E. Hess and Paula McAvoy, *The Political Classroom: Evidence and Ethics in Democratic Education* (Routledge, 2014); see also Amy Gutmann and Dennis F. Thompson, *Why Deliberative Democracy?* (Princeton University Press, 2009).
5. Timothy J. Shaffer, Nicholas V. Longo, Idit Manosevitch, and Maxine S. Thomas, eds., *Deliberative Pedagogy: Teaching and Learning for Democratic Engagement* (MSU Press, 2017).
6. Eduard Lindeman, *The Meaning of Adult Education* (New York: New Republic, Inc., 1926).
7. Eduard Lindeman, *The Meaning of Adult Education* (New York: New Republic, Inc., 1926) 9; see also 10: "experience is the adult learner's living textbook."
8. Stephen Brookfield, "The Contribution of Eduard Lindeman to the Development of Theory and Philosophy in Adult Education." *Adult Education Quarterly* 34, no. 4 (1984): 185–96.
9. See Stephen Brookfield, "The Contribution of Eduard Lindeman to the Development of Theory and Philosophy in Adult Education." *Adult Education Quarterly* 34, no. 4 (1984): 185–96; John Dewey, *The Later Works of John Dewey, The Later Works, 1925–1953: Volume 13, 1938–1939* (Carbondale: Southern Illinois University Press, 1988); Plato, *Republic*, 488a–89d.
10. John Rawls, "The Domain of the Political and Overlapping Consensus," *New York University Law Review* 64, no. 2 (May 1989).
11. See David Egan, "Is There Anything Especially Expert about Being a Philosopher?" *Aeon*, June 13, 2021, https://aeon.co/ideas/is-there-anything-especially-expert-about-being-a-philosopher.
12. See Jonathan E. Collins, "Do Teachers Want Democracy? Deliberative Culture and Teachers' Evaluations of Schools," *Urban Affairs Review* 56, no. 5 (2020): 1529–52; Kiel Francis Harell, "Practicing Democracy with Teachers: A Multicase Analysis of the Foxfire Course for Teachers" (PhD diss., The University of Wisconsin–Madison, 2016); Kiel F. Harell, "Deliberative Decision-Making in

Teacher Education," *Teaching and Teacher Education* 77 (2019): 299–308; Pat Mahony, "Should 'Ought' be Taught?" *Teaching and Teacher Education* 25, no. 7 (2009): 983–89; Emily Robertson, "Teacher Education in a Democratic Society: Learning and Teaching the Practices of Democratic Participation," *Handbook of Research on Teacher Education*, edited by Marilyn Cochran-Smith, Sharon Feiman-Nemser, D. John McIntyre, and Kelly E. Demers (Abingdon: Routledge, 2008); Sarah Marie Stitzlein, "Deliberative Democracy in Teacher Education," *Journal of Public Deliberation* 6, iss. 1, Article 5 (2010); Bryan R. Warnick and Sarah K. Silverman, "A Framework for Professional Ethics Courses in Teacher Education," *Journal of Teacher Education* 62, no. 3 (May 2011): 273–85.

13. Excellent resources for introducing these features of normative inquiry to seasoned educators are Harry Brighouse and Gina Schouten, "To Charter or not to Charter: What Questions Should We Ask, and What Will the Answers Tell Us?" *Harvard Educational Review* 84, no. 3 (2014a): 341–64; Harry Brighouse and Gina Schouten, "The Relationship Between Philosophy and Evidence in Education," *Theory and Research in Education* 13, no. 1 (2014b): 5–22.

14. Eduard Lindeman, "World Peace through Adult Education," *The Nation's Schools* 35 (1945): 23; as cited in Stephen Brookfield, "Adult Education and the Democratic Imperative: The Vision of Eduard Lindeman as a Contemporary Charter for Adult Education," *Studies in Adult Education* 15, no. 1 (1983): 36–46.

15. See for example Plato, *Gorgias* 495a, 500b; *Protagoras* 331c–d; *Republic* 346a.

CHAPTER 13

1. For a recent and brief survey of existing Ethics Bowl programs around the world and their respective reach and impact, see Lisa M. Lee, "The Growth of Ethics Bowls: A Pedagogical Tool to Develop Moral Reasoning in a Complex World," *International Journal of Ethics Education* 6, no. 1 (2021).

2. Participation data: *Association for Practical and Professional Ethics Intercollegiate Ethics Bowl: History and Overview* (2020).

3. Participation data provided by the Parr Center for Ethics.

4. For more information about this platform, see "About NHSEBOne," Parr Center for Ethics, 2021, https://nhseb.unc.edu/one.

5. For more information about NHSEBBridge program and its pedagogical approach, see "NHSEBBridge," Parr Center for Ethics, 2020, https://nhseb.unc.edu/bridge.

6. Two key examples currently exist in the Philadelphia High School Ethics Bowl hosted by the University of Pennsylvania's Project for Philosophy for the Young (see Michelle Berger, "Learning Civil Discourse and Open-Mindedness from High Schoolers," *Penn Today*, 2020, https://penntoday.upenn.edu/news/learning-civil-discourse-and-open-mindedness-high-schoolers-ethics-bowl), and the Outreach Invitational Ethics Bowl, hosted by the Center for Public Philosophy at UCSC (see Scott Rappaport, "Bringing Ethics Bowl to Underserved High Schools in Northern

California," *UCSC News Center*, 2020, https://reports.news.ucsc.edu/ethics-bowl/bringing-ethics-bowl).

7. See Michael Vazquez's chapter in this volume.

8. See Parr Center for Ethics. *National High School Ethics Bowl Participant Feedback Survey: 2019–2020.* (2020).

9. See Robert Ladenson, "Civility as Democratic Civic Virtue," in *Civility in Politics and Education*, edited by Deborah Mower and Wade Robison 207–20 (New York: Routledge, 2012).

10. See Parr Center for Ethics. *National High School Ethics Bowl Participant Feedback Survey: 2019–2020* (2020).

11. For more on this approach, see Anthony Laden's "Learning to be Equal: Just Schools as Schools of Justice," in *Education, Justice, and Democracy*, edited by Danielle Allen and Rob Reich (Chicago, IL: University of Chicago Press, 2013), 68; and *Reasoning: A Social Picture* (New York: Oxford University Press, 2012). For more on the nonpersuasive objective of the Ethics Bowl format, see Kyle Robertson's chapter in this volume.

12. For additional information and useful resources about bringing Ethics Bowl into classrooms and curricula at various grade levels, see the appendix.

13. See Roberta Israeloff and Matt Deaton, "Ethics Bowl for the Classroom," 2014.

References and Resources

CHAPTER 11

Allen, Danielle. *Education and Equality*. Chicago: University of Chicago Press, 2016.

Anderson, Elizabeth. "Democracy: Instrumental vs. Non-instrumental Value." *Contemporary Debates in Political Philosophy* (2009): 213–27.

Apple, Michael W. "Is Deliberative Democracy Enough in Teacher Education." In *Handbook of Research on Teacher Education*, edited by Marilyn Cochran-Smith, Sharon Feiman-Nemser, D. John McIntyre, and Kelly E. Demers. Abingdon: Routledge, 2008.

Brighouse, Harry, and Gina Schouten. "To Charter or not to Charter: What Questions Should We Ask, and What Will the Answers Tell Us?" *Harvard Educational Review* 84, no. 3 (2014a): 341–64.

Brighouse, Harry, and Gina Schouten. "The Relationship Between Philosophy and Evidence in Education." *Theory and Research in Education* 13, no. 1 (2014b): 5–22.

Brookfield, Stephen. "Adult Education and the Democratic Imperative: The Vision of Eduard Lindeman as a Contemporary Charter for Adult Education." *Studies in Adult Education* 15, no. 1 (1983): 36–46.

Brookfield, Stephen. "The Contribution of Eduard Lindeman to the Development of Theory and Philosophy in Adult Education." *Adult Education Quarterly* 34, no. 4 (1984): 185–96.

Butin, Dan W., ed. *Teaching Social Foundations of Education: Contexts, Theories, and Issues*. Mahwah, NJ: Lawrence Erlbaum Publishers, 2005.

Collins, Jonathan E. "Do Teachers Want Democracy? Deliberative Culture and Teachers' Evaluations of Schools." *Urban Affairs Review* 56, no. 5 (2020): 1529–52.

Cummings, Rhoda, Cleborne Maddux, Aaron Richmond, and Antonia Cladianos. "Moral Reasoning of Education Students: The Effects of Direct Instruction in Moral Development Theory and Participation in Moral Dilemma Discussion." *Teachers College Record* 112, no. 3 (2010): 621–44.

Dewey, John. *The Later Works of John Dewey, The Later Works, 1925–1953: Volume 13, 1938–1939.* Carbondale: Southern Illinois University Press, 1988.
Egan, David. "Is There Anything Especially Expert about Being a Philosopher?" Aeon, June 13, 2021. https://aeon.co/ideas/is-there-anything-especially-expert-about-being-a-philosopher.
Gutmann, Amy. *Democratic Education.* Princeton University Press, 1999.
Gutmann, Amy, and Dennis F. Thompson. *Why Deliberative Democracy?* Princeton University Press, 2009.
Harell, Kiel Francis. "Practicing Democracy with Teachers: A Multicase Analysis of the Foxfire Course for Teachers." PhD Diss., The University of Wisconsin-Madison, 2016.
Harell, Kiel F. "Deliberative Decision-Making in Teacher Education." *Teaching and Teacher Education* 77 (2019): 299–308.
Heath, Joseph. *The Machinery of Government: Public Administration and the Liberal State.* Oxford University Press, 2020.
Hess, Diana E., and Paula McAvoy. *The Political Classroom: Evidence and Ethics in Democratic Education.* Routledge, 2014.
Laden, Anthony Simon. *Reasoning: A Social Picture.* Oxford University Press, 2012.
Ladenson, Robert F. "Civility as Democratic Civic Virtue." In *Civility in Politics and Education,* edited by Deborah Mower and Wade L. Robison. New York: Routledge, 2013.
Levinson, Meira, and Jacob Fay, eds. *Democratic Discord in Schools: Cases and Commentaries in Educational Ethics.* Harvard Education Press, 2019.
Levinson, Meira, and Jacob Fay, eds. *Dilemmas of Educational Ethics: Cases and Commentaries.* Harvard Education Press, 2016.
Lindeman, Eduard. *The Meaning of Adult Education.* New York: New Republic, Inc., 1926.
Lindeman, Eduard. *What is Adult Education?* Unpublished manuscript, Columbia University, Butler Library Lindeman Archive, New York.
Lindeman, Eduard. "World Peace through Adult Education." *The Nation's Schools* 35 (1945): 23; as cited in Brookfield, Stephen (1983): 44.
Lipman, Matthew. *Thinking in Education.* Cambridge: Cambridge University Press, 1991.
Mahony, Pat. "Should 'Ought' be Taught?" *Teaching and Teacher Education* 25, no. 7 (2009): 983–89.
Mansbridge, Jane. Everyday talk in the Deliberative System. In *Deliberative Politics: Essays on Democracy and Disagreement,* edited by Stephen Macedo. Oxford University Press, 1999.
Moody, Harry R. "Philosophical Presuppositions of Education for Old Age." *Educational Gerontology* 1, no. 1 (1976): 1–16.
Parker, Walter C., and Diana Hess. "Teaching with and for Discussion." *Teaching and Teacher Education* 17, no. 3 (2001): 273–89.
Plato. *Plato: Laws 1 and 2.* Translated with Commentary by Susan Sauvé Meyer. Oxford University Press, 2015.

Rawls, John. "The Domain of the Political and Overlapping Consensus." *New York University Law Review* 64, no. 2 (May 1989).

Robertson, Emily. "Teacher Education in a Democratic Society: Learning and Teaching the Practices of Democratic Participation." In *Handbook of Research on Teacher Education*, edited by Marilyn Cochran-Smith, Sharon Feiman-Nemser, D. John McIntyre, and Kelly E. Demers. Abingdon: Routledge, 2008.

Shaffer, Timothy J., Nicholas V. Longo, Idit Manosevitch, and Maxine S. Thomas, eds. *Deliberative pedagogy: Teaching and Learning for Democratic Engagement.* MSU Press, 2017.

Shortt, D., P. Reynolds, M. McAteer, and F. Hallett. "To Believe, to Think, to Know—to Teach?" In *Philosophical Perspectives on Teacher Education,* edited by R. Heilbronn and L. Foreman-Peck. John Wiley & Sons, 2015.

Stewart, David Wood. *Adult learning in America: Eduard Lindeman and His Agenda for Lifelong Education.* RE Krieger, 1987.

Stitzlein, Sarah Marie (2010) "Deliberative Democracy in Teacher Education," *Journal of Public Deliberation* 6: iss. 1, article 5.

Warnick, Bryan R., and Sarah K. Silverman. "A Framework for Professional Ethics Courses in Teacher Education." *Journal of Teacher Education* 62, no. 3 (May 2011): 273–85.

CHAPTER 13

Association for Practical and Professional Ethics (APPE). *Association for Practical and Professional Ethics Intercollegiate Ethics Bowl: History and Overview.* (2020).

Berger, Michelle. "Learning Civil Discourse and Open-Mindedness from High Schoolers." *Penn Today*, 2020. https://penntoday.upenn.edu/news/learning-civil-discourse-and-open-mindedness-high-schoolers-ethics-bowl.

Israeloff, Roberta, and Matt Deaton. "Ethics Bowl for the Classroom." 2014. https://nhseb.unc.edu/wp-content/uploads/sites/2427/2014/06/Ethics-Bowl-for-the-Classroom.pdf.

Laden, Anthony. "Learning to Be Equal: Just Schools as Schools of Justice." In *Education, Justice, and Democracy*, edited by Danielle Allen and Rob Reich, 62–79. Chicago, IL: University of Chicago Press, 2013.

Laden, Anthony. *Reasoning: A Social Picture.* New York: Oxford University Press, 2012.

Ladenson, Robert. "Civility as Democratic Civic Virtue." In *Civility in Politics and Education*, edited by Deborah Mower and Wade Robison, 207–20. New York: Routledge, 2012.

Lee, Lisa M. "The Growth of Ethics Bowls: A Pedagogical Tool to Develop Moral Reasoning in a Complex World." *International Journal of Ethics Education* 6, no. 1 (2021): 141–48.

Parr Center for Ethics. "About NHSEBOne." 2021, https://nhseb.unc.edu/one.

Parr Center for Ethics. *National High School Ethics Bowl Participant Feedback Survey: 2019–2020* (2020).

Parr Center for Ethics. "NHSEBBridge." 2020, https://nhseb.unc.edu/bridge.
Rappaport, Scott. "Bringing Ethics Bowl to Underserved High Schools in Northern California." *UCSC News Center*, 2020. https://reports.news.ucsc.edu/ethics-bowl/bringing-ethics-bowl/.

ETHICS BOWL ORGANIZATIONS

APPE IEB (Intercollegiate Ethics Bowl): https://www.appe-ethics.org/about-ethics-bowl
Canadian High School Ethics Bowl: https://www.ethicsbowl.ca/en-ca/
National High School Ethics Bowl (NHSEB): https://nhseb.unc.edu/
Middle School Ethics Bowl (MSEB): https://www.kentplace.org/ethics-institute/student-programs/middle-school-ethics-bowl
Philosothon (Perth, Australia): https://www.philosothon.net/history.html

K–12 PHILOSOPHY RESOURCES

Philosophy Learning and Teaching Organization (PLATO): https://www.plato-philosophy.org/hs-ethics-bowl/

BOOKS, ARTICLES, AND PERIODICALS

"Civility as Democratic Civic Virtue," Robert F. Ladenson. In *Civility in Politics and Education*, edited by Deborah Mower and Wade Robison, 207–220. New York, NY: Routledge.
Ethics in Action: A Case-Based Approach by David R. Keller, Peggy Connolly, Martin G. Leever, and Becky Cox (Wiley-Blackwell), 2009.
Precollege Philosophy and Public Practice (P4): https://www.pdcnet.org/p4/Precollege-Philosophy-and-Public-Practice

ETHICS CENTERS AND PHILOSOPHY AND ETHICS ORGANIZATIONS

A2Ethics: www.a2ethics.org
American Association of Philosophy Teachers: https://philosophyteachers.org/
American Philosophical Association: https://www.apaonline.org/default.aspx
Association for Practical and Professional Ethics: https://www.appe-ethics.org/
Center for Public Philosophy—University of California Santa Cruz: https://publicphilosophy.ucsc.edu/

Kegley Institute of Ethics—California State University, Bakersfield: https://www.cs.csubak.edu/~kie/
Precollege Philosophy and Public Practice: https://www.pdcnet.org/p4/Precollege-Philosophy-and-Public-Practice
Prindle Institute for Ethics: https://www.prindleinstitute.org/
Questions: Philosophy for Young People: https://www.pdcnet.org/questions/Questions:-Philosophy-for-Young-People
Society for Ethics Across the Curriculum: https://www.seac-online.org/resources/

About the Editors and Contributors

William M. Beals teaches philosophy at Stanford Online High School. He cocoaches Stanford Online's Ethics Bowl team and primarily teaches eleventh and twelfth year core philosophy classes. His philosophical interests are mainly in ethics, moral psychology, and the philosophy of action, with a significant side-interest in Nietzsche and metaethics. Will received his BA in philosophy from Colgate University in 2002 and his PhD in philosophy from Stanford University in 2012.

Peggy Connolly served eighteen years on the National Intercollegiate Ethics Bowl Case Writing Committee, and as chair for ten. She served on the Institution Review Boards of Northwestern University, Illinois Mathematics and Science Academy, Central DuPage Healthcare System, and on Central DuPage Hospital's Ethics Committee for nearly two decades. She is a Fellow of the American Association for the Advancement of Science, and former president of the National Association of Academies of Science. MIT's Lincoln Laboratory named Asteroid #21445 "Pegconnolly" for her work with science research students. She's the author of several publications, including coauthoring *Ethics in Action: A Case-Based Approach*.

Andrew Cullison, founding Executive Director of The Cincinnati Ethics Center at the University of Cincinnati, was the Director of the Janet Prindle Institute for Ethics at DePauw University and Associate Professor of Philosophy. He was on DePauw's first Ethics Bowl team as a student in 1999, and he has coached Ethics Bowl teams at every institution he was affiliated with after that, before returning to DePauw. As director of the Prindle Institute, he started the annual Indiana High School Ethics Bowl in 2014 and the annual National Summer High School Ethics Bowl Invitational in 2019.

Christina Drogalis teaches philosophy at Stanford Online High School. She cocoaches Stanford Online's Ethics Bowl team and primarily teaches eleventh and twelfth grade core philosophy classes. Her research interests include ethics, and particularly questions about moral improvement and education in the work of Immanuel Kant. Christina earned her BA in philosophy and political science from the University of Scranton in 2008 and her MA and PhD in philosophy from Loyola University Chicago in 2013.

Richard Greene is a professor of philosophy at Weber State University. He is the director of the Richard Richards Institute for Ethics, and is a past director of the Intercollegiate Ethics Bowl. He is the author of *Spoiler Alert! It's a Book about the Philosophy of Spoilers*. He has edited eighteen books on philosophy and pop culture. He is one of the hosts of the pop culture and philosophy podcast *I Think, Therefore I Fan*.

Roberta Israeloff has directed the Squire Family Foundation since its founding in 2007. The foundation advocates for and supports innovative philosophy initiatives in K–12 classrooms as well as other nontraditional settings. The foundation is also a cofounder of the Philosophy Learning and Teaching Organization (PLATO) and the National High School Ethics Bowl (NHSEB). Author of over a dozen books, she is also an editor and writing teacher.

Connie Krosney is a retired professor of education. Her areas of focus, for thirty-five years, were the social foundations of education, especially sociology, applied ethics, and adult development. She has served on the Mount Tamalpais College (formerly Prison University Project) Board since 2015. She has volunteered as a tutor for the college program at San Quentin, and served on the faculty and as an Ethics Bowl coach. She is a strong advocate for liberal arts education and the use of dialogue in all educational settings. connie.krosney@gmail.com

Robert F. Ladenson is Professor of Philosophy Emeritus at the Illinois Institute of Technology. He created the Ethics Bowl, and from 1997 to 2009 was principal organizer and developer of the Association for Practical and Professional Ethics Intercollegiate Ethics Bowl (APPE IEB). For twenty years (1987–2007) he was a special education due process hearing officer in Illinois, a position in which he heard cases involving disputes between parents of children with disabilities and public school districts under federal and state special education laws. He is the author of *Moral Issues in Special Education: An Inquiry into the Basic Rights, Responsibilities, and Ideals* (2020).

Jana Mohr Lone is the Executive Director of PLATO (Philosophy Learning and Teaching Organization) and affiliate associate professor of philosophy at the University of Washington. She is the author of *Seen and Not Heard* (2021) and *The Philosophical Child* (2012), coauthor of *Philosophy in Education: Questioning and Dialogue in Schools* (2016), coeditor of *Philosophy and Education: Introducing Philosophy to Young People* (2012), and the author of many articles about young people's philosophical thinking. She is the founding editor of the journal *Questions: Philosophy for Young People.*

Marcia A. McKelligan is professor of philosophy at DePauw University, where she has taught since 1976. Her areas of teaching and scholarly interest include seventeenth- and eighteenth-century Continental and British philosophy; philosophical cosmology; conceptual, metaphysical, and axiological questions about death; and recently, biomedical ethics. She has coached the DePauw University Ethics Bowl team since 1999 and its Bioethics Bowl team since 2012. She has guided her students to two national and several regional championships. She is also a frequent judge at Intercollegiate and High School Ethics Bowl competitions and has authored cases for the national Bioethics Bowl competition.

Karen Mizell is Professor of Philosophy at Utah Valley University and Director of the Ethics Minor and Ethics Certificate programs. Her primary areas of teaching and research are Ethics, Philosophy of Education, Philosophy of Law, Philosophy of Childhood, Philosophy for Children, and Animal/Human Relationships. Karen joined the faculty of Utah Valley University with prior appointments at Brigham Young University (visiting appointment), Clayton State College, and University of Oklahoma. She is founder and past director of the Utah High School Ethics Bowl, cofounder of the Wasatch Regional Ethics Bowl, and is the recipient of several teaching and service awards, including the State of Utah Award for Excellence in Service-Learning.

Kathleen J. Richards is an attorney who represents incarcerated people at their parole hearings. Previously, she practiced family law, often as court-appointed attorney for minors in high-conflict custody cases, and dependency law. Since 2015, Kathy has been a member of the faculty at Mount Tamalpais College, a college program located inside San Quentin State Prison in California. In 2017, Kathy began coaching the Ethics Bowl team inside San Quentin with Kyle Robertson from the Center for Public Philosophy at UC Santa Cruz. Kathy also serves on the Board of the Sonoma Speakers Series and coaches her local high-school's Mock Trial Team. kathy@kjr-jd.com

Alex M. Richardson is director of the National High School Ethics Bowl (NHSEB), headquartered at the University of North Carolina's Parr Center for Ethics in Chapel Hill. He also teaches in the Department of Philosophy at Elon University. Working at the intersections of ethics, political philosophy, and the philosophy of education, Alex is an award-winning teacher and a strong advocate for public and precollege philosophy pedagogy.

Kyle Robertson is a lecturer in the UC Santa Cruz philosophy department. In 2015 he cofounded the Center for Public Philosophy at UC Santa Cruz. An attorney, he has a passion for all things public philosophy. He is involved with high school Ethics Bowl programs, teaching as part of Mount Tamalpais College in San Quentin State Prison, and philosophy for children. He regularly speaks on public philosophy and publishes on the challenges of doing public philosophy.

Rachel Robison-Greene is an assistant professor of philosophy at Utah State University. Her research interests include the nature of personhood and the self, animal minds and animal ethics, environmental ethics, and ethics and technology. She sits on both the Diversity and Rules Committees for the National Intercollegiate Ethics Bowl. She is a cofounder of the Utah Prison Ethics Bowl Project, which is a program that brings ethics education and debate into the Wasatch and Timpanogos prisons. She regularly writes public philosophy articles for *The Prindle Post* and is the author of *Edibility and In Vitro Meat: Ethical Considerations*.

Wendy C. Turgeon teaches philosophy at St. Joseph's College-NY and has been active in precollege philosophy for many years. Her most recent publication is the book *Philosophical Adventures with Fairy Tales* (Rowman & Littlefield, 2020), a guide to exploring the philosophical concepts found in these familiar but still mysterious stories. She has served as a judge for the Long Island Ethics Bowl competition since its inception and remains forever impressed by the students and their coaches, who dedicate countless hours to preparing the cases. wturgeon@sjcny.edu

Michael Vazquez is teaching assistant professor and Director of Outreach in the Department of Philosophy and the Parr Center for Ethics, UNC-Chapel Hill. He also serves as a summer lecturer on the Social Foundations of Education for Penn's Midcareer Doctoral Program in Educational Leadership. Michael is committed to forging lasting, democratic, and collaborative partnerships between the academy and the community and to cultivating the philosophical voices of people of all ages. His research interests span ancient philosophy, ethics, philosophy of education, and democratic theory. As an educator he specializes in experiential education, precollege pedagogy, learning across the lifespan, and civic education. Michael.vazquez@unc.edu

Morgan E. Wallhagen teaches philosophy at Stanford Online High School. Morgan helped found the Ethics Bowl team at Stanford Online in 2015 which he cocoaches. He works primarily in the philosophy of mind and philosophy of cognitive science with a focus on consciousness, though he is broadly interested in metaphysics and epistemology. His publications include, "Consciousness and Action: Does Cognitive Science Support (Mild) Epiphenomenalism?" *British Journal for the Philosophy of Science,* 2007; "On Carruthers' Argument for Higher-Order Representationalism," *Southwest Philosophical Studies,* 2007; and "Mental States as Presentations," *Southwest Philosophical Studies,* 2013.

www.ingramcontent.com/pod-product-compliance
Lightning Source LLC
Chambersburg PA
CBHW030141240426
43672CB00005B/213